CASE STUDIES IN SPECIAL EDUCATION LAW

No Child Left Behind Act and Individuals with Disabilities Education Improvement Act

MARY KONYA WEISHAAR
Southern Illinois University Edwardsville

PEARSON

Merrill
Prentice Hall

Upper Saddle River, New Jersey
Columbus, Ohio

Library of Congress Cataloging-in-Publication Data

Weishaar, Mary Ellen.
  Case studies in special education law : No Child Left Behind Act and Individuals with Disabilities Education Improvement Act / Mary Konya Weishaar.
    p. cm.
  Includes index.
  ISBN 0-13-218628-4 (pbk.)
  1. Special education—Law and legislation—United States. 2. Children with disabilities—Education—Law and legislation—United States. 3. Special education—United States—Case studies. 4. Children with disabilities—Education—United States—Case studies. 5. United States. No Child Left Behind Act of 2001. 6. United States. Individuals with Disabilities Education Improvement Act of 2004. I. Title.
  KF4209.3.W45 2007
  344.73'0791—dc22

                                                            2006012119

Vice President and Executive Publisher: Jeffery W. Johnston
Executive Editor: Ann Castel Davis
Editorial Assistant: Penny Burleson
Production Editor: Sheryl Glicker Langner
Production Coordination: Thistle Hill Publishing Services, LLC
Design Coordinator: Diane C. Lorenzo
Cover Designer: Jason Moore
Cover Image: Corbis
Production Manager: Laura Messerly
Director of Marketing: David Gesell
Marketing Manager: Amy Judd
Marketing Coordinator: Brian Mounts

This book was set in Bookman by Integra Software Services.

Pearson Education Ltd.
Pearson Education Singapore Pte. Ltd.
Pearson Education Canada, Ltd.
Pearson Education–Japan

Pearson Education Australia Pty. Limited
Pearson Education North Asia Ltd.
Pearson Educación de Mexico, S.A. de C.V.
Pearson Education Malaysia Pte. Ltd.

ISBN 0-13-218628-4

Thanks to my family—Phil, Paul, Mark, Pat, and Joe—for encouraging me and supporting me during this project. I also appreciate the assistance and insight given by Dr. Victoria Groves Scott, a master teacher and parent.

Preface

President George W. Bush made the following remarks as he signed the Individuals with Disabilities Education Improvement Act of 2004:

> America's schools educate over 6 million children with disabilities. In the past, those students were too often just shuffled through the system with little expectation that they could make significant progress or succeed like their fellow classmates. Children with disabilities deserve high hopes, high expectations, and extra help. . . . In the bill I sign today, we're raising expectations for the students. We're giving schools and parents the tools they need to meet them. We're applying the reforms of the No Child Left Behind Act to the Individuals with Disabilities Education Improvement Act so schools are accountable for teaching every single child. . . . All students in America can learn. That's what all of us up here believe. All of us understand we have an obligation to make sure no child is left behind in America.*

These remarks reflect a focus on higher academic expectations for children with disabilities and holding schools accountable for the achievement of students with disabilities.

The Individuals with Disabilities Education Improvement Act of 2004 (and its predecessor, the Education of All Handicapped Children Act of 1975) has been largely successful in providing *access* to public school programs for all children with disabilities. (*Note:* In this textbook, IDEA refers to the 2004 reauthorization.) The No Child Left Behind Act signed into law in 2002 (the most recent reauthorization of the Elementary and Secondary Education Act of 1965) focused on *outcomes* for all students, including those who have disabilities. Since the mid-1980s, a strong school reform movement has shifted from a focus on inputs and access to the public school system to outcomes or outputs. At the junction between the Individuals with Disabilities Education Improvement Act and the No Child

*Bush, G. W. (2004, December 3). *President's Remarks at the Signing of H. R. 1350.* Retrieved from the White House Web site (*http://www.whitehouse.gov/news/releases/2004/12/20041203-6.html*).

Left Behind legislation are questions about how "access" and "outcomes" can work together for the improvement of all students. To understand some of the difficult issues involved, consider the following scenarios.

Scenario 1

A recent newspaper article reported that the local elementary school was identified for improvement because a subgroup, students with disabilities, had not met the standard for adequate yearly progress (the state-defined time line based on the state assessment for ensuring that all children were proficient in reading and mathematics by 2013–2014). The public was outraged that one subgroup could determine that the school needed improvement. In fact, the school superintendent wrote many letters to legislators expressing discontent that students in special education had to take the state test. He proposed excluding students in special education from taking the state test and stated that their individualized education programs (IEPs) should suffice in showing progress. He stated that some students in special education had never taken a standardized test before, weren't even working in the same curriculum as most students, and would never fully meet the standards.

Scenario 2

The parent of John, who has autism and a health impairment, was sent a letter from John's school stating that the school was in its second year of not meeting adequate yearly progress. The letter stated that parents could elect to transfer their children to a higher performing school within the school district. When the parent contacted the superintendent's office to inquire about the possibility of John being transferred, she was told that the only other higher performing school in the district did not have the special education services that John required in his individualized education program.

Scenario 3

Jamie was a high school student with significant learning disabilities. He was placed in a special education class primarily focused on independent living skills and community living skills. Jamie's parents were very pleased with his progress and the school until a recent IEP meeting, where they were told that Jamie had to take the state standardized test in reading and mathematics. Jamie had not been exposed to taking standardized tests or high school level content and could not read anywhere close to grade level. When Jamie's parents questioned members of the IEP team, they were told that only 1% of the students who had significant cognitive impairments were taking an alternate assessment and that Jamie did not have a significant cognitive impairment. Therefore, he would just have to take the test.

Although these scenarios sound far-fetched, they are not. They represent the difficulties in applying a single set of standards to all children and, at the same time, individualizing programs for some children—that is, children with disabilities.

The intent of this text is to provide students with real-life case studies that address important issues within these two laws. Students will see both best practice and less than best practice as they read the cases. The intended audience for this text is the student who is taking a course in special education law and/or administration. Often, these students are special and regular education teachers or administrators pursuing additional expertise in special education law.

Two types of questions are posed at the end of each case: *legal issues* and *other issues*. *Legal issues* pose questions about specific legal issues and dilemmas within the case, and the *other issues* pose questions that address more general issues embedded within the case. Also included is an optional activity that actively engages the student and enhances learning. Questions posed are intended to be challenging so that students are exposed to the difficulties of making judgments within the context of the ever-changing legal aspects of special education.

After reading a case, students should first determine the important legal issues involved and then answer the questions at the end of the case. For some questions, there may be more than one "correct" answer. It is essential that students engage in critical thinking and discussion when answering the questions. To answer some questions, further research of federal and state statutes, regulations, and case law may be necessary.

This text is intended to provide supplemental instruction using real-life cases while studying the law. Although chapter 1 provides an overview of each law, it is not intended to provide all details contained in each law. Students are urged to consult the resources listed at the end of chapter 1, a comprehensive law text, and their state special education statutes and regulations for all details.

Acknowledgments

I appreciate the encouragement and support of my editor, Allyson Sharp, and editorial assistant, Kathy Burk. I also appreciate the valuable and constructive feedback from my field reviewers: Betty Ashbaker, Brigham Young University; Richard Belcastro, Waynesburg College; Steven C. Camron, Eastern Michigan University; Denise E. Maricle, Southern Connecticut State University; and Malcolm L. Van Blerkom, University of Pittsburgh at Johnstown.

About the Author

Mary Konya Weishaar is associate professor in special education and associate dean of the School of Education at Southern Illinois University Edwardsville. She is the author or coauthor of five case study texts in the areas of legal and administrative issues in special education, assessment, and characteristics of children with disabilities. She has also authored several journal articles in special education and was the recipient of a Fulbright Senior Scholar Award to lecture at a university in Kiev, Ukraine. Dr. Weishaar was a special education teacher and administrator for 18 years prior to her university experience.

Discover the Merrill Resources for Special Education Website

Technology is a constantly growing and changing aspect of our field that is creating a need for new content and resources. To address this emerging need, Merrill Education has developed an online learning environment for students, teachers, and professors alike to complement our products—the *Merrill Resources for Special Education* Website. This content-rich website provides additional resources specific to this book's topic and will help you—professors, classroom teachers, and students—augment your teaching, learning, and professional development.

Our goal with this initiative is to build on and enhance what our products already offer. For this reason, the content for our user-friendly website is organized by topic and provides teachers, professors, and students with a variety of meaningful resources all in one location. With this website, we bring together the best of what Merrill has to offer: text resources, video clips, web links, tutorials, and a wide variety of information on topics of interest to general and special educators alike. Rich content, applications, and competencies further enhance the learning process.

The *Merrill Resources for Special Education* Website includes:

- Video clips specific to each topic, with questions to help you evaluate the content and make crucial theory-to-practice connections.
- Thought-provoking critical analysis questions that students can answer and turn in for evaluation or that can serve as basis for class discussions and lectures.
- Access to a wide variety of resources related to classroom strategies and methods, including lesson planning and classroom management.

* Information on all the most current relevant topics related to special and general education, including CEC and Praxis[TM] standards, IEPs, portfolios, and professional development.
* Extensive web resources and overviews on each topic addressed on the website.
* A search feature to help access specific information quickly.

To take advantage of these and other resources, please visit the *Merrill Resources for Special Education* Website at

http://www.prenhall.com/weishaar

Brief Contents

Contents

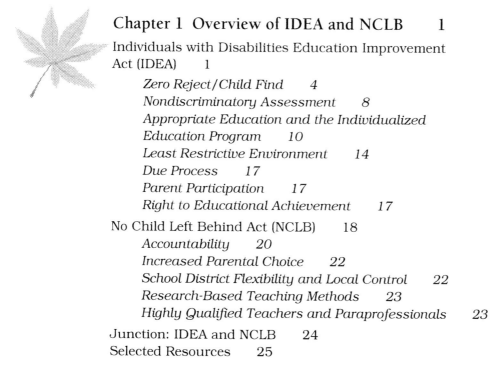

Overview of IDEA and NCLB

To fully appreciate the complicated issues involved at the intersection of the Individuals with Disabilities Education Improvement Act (IDEA) and the No Child Left Behind Act (NCLB), one must become familiar with the principles of each law. Following is an overview of each law and its founding principles.

Individuals with Disabilities Education Improvement Act (IDEA)

The roots of IDEA go back to 1975, when Congress originally passed the Education of All Handicapped Children Act. Later renamed the Individuals with Disabilities Education Act (IDEA), the law provided federal funds to states and to local education agencies (LEAs) if they complied with the conditions specified in the law and its regulations. The general purpose of the IDEA was to ensure that all children with disabilities received a free appropriate public education (FAPE) and were not discriminated against by any public school or by any agency representing the public school. The IDEA mandated that school districts provide appropriate educational services to students who had at least one of 13 specified disabilities (see Figure 1.1). The Education of All Handicapped Children Act and then the IDEA were revised and amended by Congress in 1978, 1986, 1990, 1997, and 2004. Some of the important changes included the following:

1986

* Early intervention services for infants and toddlers (birth through age 3) were added, and funding was made available to states to provide services.

Autism
Deaf-blindness
Deafness
Emotional disturbance
Hearing impairment
Learning disability
Mental retardation
Multiple disabilities
Orthopedic impairment
Other health impairment
Speech or language impairment
Traumatic brain injury
Visual impairment

FIGURE 1.1 IDEA: Thirteen
Categories of Disabilities

* The Handicapped Children's Protection Act was incorporated into the law, essentially allowing parents who prevailed in a due process hearing or lawsuit to recover attorneys' fees.

1990

* The term "handicapped student" was changed to "student with a disability" throughout the law.
* The law was renamed the "Individuals with Disabilities Education Act."
* Traumatic brain injury and autism were included as new categories of disabilities.
* School districts were required to address transition planning and services within the student's individualized education program (IEP) when the student reached the age of 16.
* Assistive technology was added as a related service.

1997

* Procedures addressing discipline of students with disabilities were added for the first time.
* IEP team membership mandated the participation of the general education teacher.
* Students with disabilities were to be included in state and school district assessments as determined by the IEP team.
* IEP goals and objectives/benchmarks had to be measurable.
* States had to offer free voluntary mediation as a method of resolving conflict.

2004

* The IDEA was renamed "Individuals with Disabilities Education Improvement Act."
* Many references were made to the No Child Left Behind Act in an effort to emphasize "outcomes" over "access" and academic achievement of all children.
* Complaints that could lead to a due process hearing were given a statute of limitation of 2 years before the date the parent or school district knew or should have known about the alleged violation of law.
* Discipline procedures were simplified.
* Informal dispute resolution strategies (e.g., voluntary mediation, mandatory resolution meeting) were strengthened and agreements were to be legally binding.
* Eligibility for learning disability could be based on lack of response to research-based intervention, not just on severe discrepancy between ability and achievement.
* With parental agreement, IEPs could be changed and amended without conducting a formal IEP meeting, and mandated members could be excused from participation.
* Short-term objectives/benchmarks were eliminated for all children except those with severe disabilities.

The most significant changes to the IDEA occurred in 1997 and 2004, when the IDEA was aligned with reform legislation for all public schools, resulting in a movement for improvement in the education of *all* students—school reform was focused on goals for all children, curriculum was aligned with the goals, and assessment was conducted to determine if students were reaching the goals. In a similar way, the IDEA focused on goals, curriculum, and assessment. Accountability and student outcomes became a focus for all students with disabilities, as well as for students in the regular education environment. States were required to develop goals for children with disabilities that were consistent with goals for all children. Children with disabilities were required to take state and districtwide assessments to assess progress toward goals. In addition, each child's individualized education program (IEP) had to be designed for progress in the general education curriculum.

Although the IDEA was revised several times, the original purpose remained unchanged: to provide a free appropriate public education (FAPE) to all children who have disabilities. Achieving this goal was originally based on six basic principles: zero reject/child find, nondiscriminatory assessment, appropriate education and the individualized education program (IEP), least restrictive environment (LRE), due process, and parent participation. A seventh principle, the right to educational achievement, emerged after reauthorization of the IDEA in 2004. (See Figure 1.2.) These principles and some important details are summarized next.

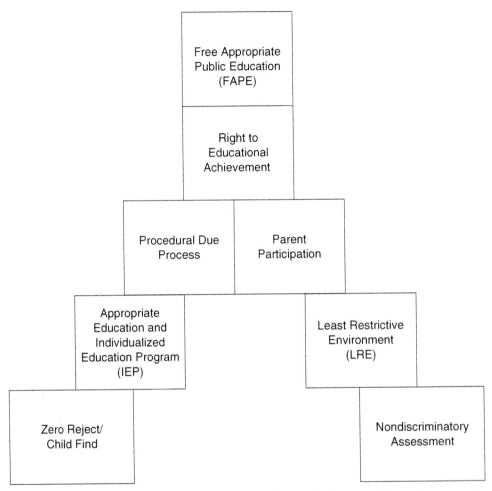

FIGURE 1.2 Principles of the IDEA: Building Blocks to a Free Appropriate
Public Education (FAPE)
Source: Adapted from *Inclusive Educational Administration: A Case Study
Approach* (p. 27), by M. K. Weishaar & J. C. Borsa, reissued 2004, Long Grove, IL:
Waveland Press.

Zero Reject/Child Find

The first principle includes both zero reject and child find. *Zero reject*
means that a school district cannot exclude a child with a disability from
FAPE, including students who have been expelled for disciplinary reasons.
Zero reject was most often associated with two scenarios: refusal of
schools to serve students with the most severe disabilities, and discipline
of students with disabilities.

During the earlier years of the law, the focus of zero reject was to "open the schoolhouse doors" to children with disabilities. Congress found that more than 1 million children with disabilities were routinely excluded from public schools. School districts had to provide a free appropriate public education to all children with disabilities, regardless of the severity or nature of the disability. Following is an illustrative example:

> James, a 10-year-old child who is profoundly deaf, moves into a small rural community with one elementary school. Although James can be integrated into the regular classroom for some subjects, he must receive special instruction for reading and language arts. In addition, James must have a sign language interpreter with him in the regular education environment. James's new school district does not have a teacher of the deaf or a sign language interpreter, and it would be very costly to create a new classroom for James. However, the zero reject principle means that James must be provided with a free appropriate public education, at whatever cost to the school district. The new school district could employ a teacher and interpreter for James, or possibly transport James to a neighboring school district where his special needs could be met, but the district of residence would be responsible for FAPE.

Discipline was not addressed in the IDEA until the 1997 reauthorization. Prior to 1997, school districts relied on case law, state law, and "best practice" in disciplining students with disabilities. Then in 1997, Congress codified into law complex detailed procedures for discipline, much of which reflected the U.S. Supreme Court decision *Honig v. Doe* (479 U.S. 1084, 1988).

In 2004, Congress again changed the procedures for disciplining students with disabilities, simplifying the process and allowing for judgment on a case-by-case basis, even for so-called "zero tolerance" state laws. Generally, building administrators can suspend students with disabilities for up to and including 10 days without invoking the special education placement change procedures. Suspensions beyond 10 consecutive days must involve the specialized convening of the IEP team to determine the relationship of the behavior to the student's disability. It is important to note that the rights for students with disabilities may apply to students who have not yet been identified as having a disability. In other words, the IDEA may apply to a student if school district (LEA—i.e., local education agency) personnel had knowledge that the student had a disability before the behavior that resulted in the discipline action occurred. General procedures for discipline and definitions of terms may be found in Figures 1.3 through 1.6.

Child find, the other aspect of this IDEA principle, means that the school district must locate, identify, and evaluate unserved and

Change of placement: Removal from school for more than 10 consecutive school days.

Interim alternative educational setting (IAES): An alternative placement that must be selected to enable the child to continue to progress in the general curriculum (in another setting) and to continue to receive services that will enable the child to meet IEP goals; must include services to address the behavior that is the subject of the discipline and must be designed to prevent the behavior from reoccurring.

Manifestation determination: An IEP meeting whose purpose is to determine whether a relationship exists between the behavior resulting in discipline and the child's disability.

The IEP team reviews:

- Child's IEP
- Teacher observation
- Any relevant information provided by the parents

The IEP team determines:

- Was the conduct caused by or did it have a relationship to the child's disability?
- Was the conduct the direct result of the LEA's failure to implement the IEP?

If either applies to the child, the conduct shall be a manifestation of the child's disability.

Functional behavioral assessment (FBA): Used in IDEA (2004), but not defined; could be considered as an assessment of the antecedent and consequences of the behavior that is subject to the discipline.

Behavioral intervention plan (BIP): Used in IDEA (2004), but not defined; could be considered as appropriate strategies and supports written as part of the IEP designed to address the problem behavior and to prevent it from reoccurring.

FIGURE 1.3 Definitions: Discipline

Source: Adapted from *Inclusive Educational Administration: A Case Study Approach* (p. 174), by M. K. Weishaar & J. C. Borsa, reissued 2004, Long Grove, IL: Waveland Press.

underserved children with disabilities. An example of child find would be when the local school district holds annual early childhood screenings. The 2004 amendments to the IDEA expanded child find requirements in private schools and among homeless students and wards of the state.

LEA may suspend or place in IAES for 10 school days or less (determined on case-by-case basis—no FBA, BIP, manifestation determination; no provision of services).

LEA wants to suspend more than 10 days (change in placement).

Must hold manifestation determination.

Review: All relevant information in child's file, including:

- Child's IEP
- Teacher observation
- Any relevant information provided by parents

To determine:

- Was conduct caused by or did it have a direct & substantial relationship to child's disability?
- Was conduct the direct result of the LEA's failure to implement the IEP?

If either applies to the child, conduct shall be a manifestation of the child's disability.

If conduct is not a manifestation of child's disability, LEA can apply same discipline as used with children who are not disabled, and for same duration. If appropriate, conduct FBA and BIP. However, child must continue to receive FAPE—to enable child to participate in the general education curriculum, although in another setting, and to progress toward IEP goals.

If conduct is a manifestation of child's disability, IEP team shall:

- Conduct FBA and implement BIP if not already conducted
- If BIP exists, review the plan and modify it as necessary to address the behavior

Child returns to the current placement unless parent and LEA agree to another placement after 10-day suspension.

FIGURE 1.4 Discipline: General Misbehavior

Source: Adapted from *Inclusive Educational Administration: A Case Study Approach* (p. 177), by M. K. Weishaar & J. C. Borsa, reissued 2004, Long Grove, IL: Waveland Press.

If student possesses or carries a weapon to school or on school grounds or to a school function . . .

OR

If student knowingly possesses or uses illegal drugs, or sells or solicits the sale of a controlled substance at school or on school grounds or at a school function . . .

OR

If student has inflicted serious bodily injury upon another person at school, on school premises, or at a school function . . .

↓

LEA can remove student to IAES for 45 school days regardless of whether behavior is determined to be a manifestation of the disability.

↓

LEA must notify parent of the decision to place in an IAES.

↓

IAES is determined by the IEP team.

↓

School day 46: Student returns to the previous placement unless LEA and parent agree otherwise or a court order extends IAES.

FIGURE 1.5 Discipline: Special Circumstances
Source: Adapted from *Inclusive Educational Administration: A Case Study Approach* (p. 180), by M. K. Weishaar & J. C. Borsa, reissued 2004, Long Grove, IL: Waveland Press.

Nondiscriminatory Assessment

The second principle, *nondiscriminatory assessment,* means that students who are evaluated as suspected of having a disability must receive a comprehensive and individualized evaluation that incorporates the following principles:

*   Persons from more than one discipline must be included in the evaluation, including someone knowledgeable in the area of the child's suspected disability.
*   Assessments cannot discriminate on the basis of race, culture, native language, or disability.

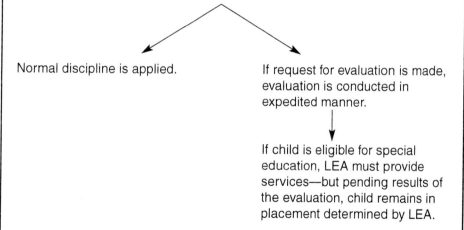

Student in regular education can assert any protections for students with disabilities if LEA had knowledge that the child has a disability before behavior that resulted in discipline action occurred.

Basis of knowledge:
- Parent expressed concern in writing, to supervisory or administrative personnel of LEA or teacher of child, that child was in need of special education.
- Parent requested an evaluation of the child.
- Teacher of the child, or other LEA personnel, had expressed specific concerns about a pattern of behavior demonstrated by the child directly to the director of special education or to supervisory personnel.

(Note: LEA did not have knowledge if the parent did not allow an evaluation OR refused special education services OR if child was evaluated and found ineligible for special education.)

Normal discipline is applied.

If request for evaluation is made, evaluation is conducted in expedited manner.

If child is eligible for special education, LEA must provide services—but pending results of the evaluation, child remains in placement determined by LEA.

FIGURE 1.6   Discipline: Student Not in Special Education Misbehaves

- A variety of assessments and procedures must be used.
- The child must be assessed in all areas of suspected disability.
- Assessments must be valid and reliable.

Consider the following example as an illustration of this principle:

Tamisha, a 3rd-grade student, moved to an urban school district in New York City. The school psychologist who evaluated her administered an achievement test that was primarily normed on white, middle

*class children. This test was invalid because Tamisha's background
and experiences were not represented within the norm group.*

One important change in the 2004 reauthorization of the IDEA
involved the identification of learning disability. School districts were
allowed to opt out of the federal regulation mandating a written report
that specified a student could be made eligible for learning disabilities
where "there is a severe discrepancy between achievement and ability that
is not correctable without special education and related services." This
has been a basic element of learning disability eligibility criteria since
1978. Beginning in July 2004, however, school districts were able to use a
process involving a "response to scientifically based interventions" model
as part of the evaluation. For example, at one time a child who had the
following test profile would not likely have been eligible for the category of
learning disability because there was not a severe discrepancy between
achievement and ability:

* IQ of 80
* Standard score on an achievement test: reading – 79, mathematics – 82, spelling – 78

If the same school district opted to use a process involving response to
scientifically based interventions, this child would have been involved in a
prereferral process where several specialized reading, written language,
and mathematics interventions were attempted over a period of time and
the child's progress tracked. If the child did not respond to these scientifically or research-based interventions, the child would have been referred
and likely qualify as learning disabled. The issue of severe discrepancy
between ability and achievement would not have been a factor in determining the child's eligibility for special education. Therefore, the same
child could have received special education and related services. The law
also prohibits states from enforcing the severe discrepancy model.

Appropriate Education and the Individualized
Education Program

The third principle, *appropriate education and the individualized education
program* (IEP), is based on a document developed annually using a specified process by a group of professionals, including the parents.
Essentially, the IEP (or for infants and toddlers, the individualized family
service plan, IFSP) is a blueprint of services necessary to meet the child's
needs to enable him or her to successfully progress toward individual
goals (and objectives, for children who take alternate assessments aligned
to alternate achievement standards) that have been set for the child. An
IEP provides evidence that a child is receiving a free appropriate public
education (FAPE). This means that children with disabilities are entitled to

a public education, at no cost to the parents, that is appropriate to meet their individual needs. The IEP amounts to a commitment of the school district's resources for providing FAPE.

Participants at the IEP meeting include the following:

* The child's parents
* Regular education teacher (if the child is, or may be, participating in the regular education environment)
* Special education teacher
* School district representative who is qualified to provide or supervise special education, is knowledgeable about the general education curriculum, and can commit district resources
* Person who can interpret the instructional implications of the evaluation results
* Other persons at the discretion of the parent or school district
* The child, where appropriate

It can be noted that there are provisions in the IDEA to excuse a member of the IEP team from attending the meeting under certain circumstances if the parent and district official agree in writing to the excusal.

Specific components of the IEP are listed below along with illustrative examples.

1. *Present levels of academic achievement and functional performance:* This statement must include a description of how the child's disability affects his or her involvement and progress in the general education curriculum.

   Carlos, a 10th-grade student with significant learning disabilities, might have the following statement included as part of the IEP: "Carlos has difficulty decoding and writing words. He often recognizes the beginning and ending sounds of words, but is unable to decode the middle sounds. Carlos is unable to read more than two or three words in a minute using 3rd-grade materials, and he often becomes frustrated. His peers read fluently at a rate of 100 words per minute in 10th-grade level materials. When content area printed materials are read aloud to Carlos, he comprehends at least 85% to 90% of the material. Carlos' struggle to decode words affects his progress in the general education curriculum."

2. *Measurable annual goals, including academic and functional goals:* These goals are designed to meet the child's needs resulting from his or her disability and enable the child to be involved in and progress in the general education curriculum.

   Two goals for Carlos might include the following: "By May 20, given a list of 20 words with a pattern of consonant-vowel-consonant, Carlos will read the list aloud at 80% accuracy. By May 20, Carlos will be able to read a list of 10 items needed from the grocery store and locate the items at 100% accuracy without prompts."

3. *Benchmarks or short-term objectives (needed only if the child takes alternate assessments aligned to alternate achievement standards):* Benchmarks or short-term objectives break down the measurable goal into measurable intermediate pieces.

   In Carlos's case, he does not take alternate assessments aligned to alternate achievement standards, so he does not have short-term objectives or benchmarks.

4. *Description of how the child's progress toward the annual goals will be measured and when periodic reports on the progress will be provided:* The reports can be scheduled to coincide with reporting periods used with all students, such as quarterly reports or semester reports.

   For Carlos, the statement might read: "Carlos's progress will be measured by administering a reading assessment listing common items in the community on a weekly basis. Results will be graphed and will be shared with his parents at the end of each quarter."

5. *Special education, related services, supplementary aids and services:* Services indicated must be based on peer-reviewed research as much as possible and include a statement of program modifications and supports for school personnel. Services must also advance the child toward attaining annual goals, help the child to be involved in and make progress in the general education curriculum, help the child to participate in extracurricular and other nonacademic activities, and help the child to be educated and participate with other children who do not have disabilities.

   Carlos might need the following services: "Carlos will participate in the general education curriculum by taking courses in prealgebra, civics, and biology. He will attend a special education resource room during the last hour of each day, where assignments and texts will be read aloud and homework completed. A paraprofessional will be placed in the regular education environment and will assist Carlos with written assignments and reading. Carlos will attend a special education reading instruction program provided by the special education teacher."

6. *The extent, if any, to which the child will not participate with nondisabled children in the regular class and in nonacademic/extracurricular activities:* The assumption in this statement is that children will participate in the regular education environment—and if not, a statement must justify why the child is not participating.

   This statement might be included on Carlos's IEP: "Carlos will participate in the regular education environment for all classes except reading and a support class because of his significant need for small group instruction in reading and support in completing assigned tasks. He will also participate on the school soccer team."

7. *Statement of individual appropriate accommodations that are necessary to measure the academic achievement and functional performance of the child on state and districtwide assessments:* If the IEP team decides that the child should take an alternate assessment, there must be a statement specifying why the child cannot participate in the regular assessment and what assessment will be used.

   "Carlos will take the state assessment with the following accommodations: extended time for test, testing in an alternate environment (special education classroom), and tests in areas other than reading are to be read aloud to him."

8. *Date for the beginning of services and modifications, anticipated frequency, location and duration of services:* This information must be clearly specified to show when services will begin, where the services will occur, and how often and how long the services will be given.

   For Carlos, the following might be written:

   Date of initiation of services and modifications: Beginning of school year (September 4)

   Anticipated frequency: Daily when school is in session

   Location of services: Individual aide providing support within the regular education environment; special reading class and support class provided in the special education resource room

   Duration: End of school year (May 30)

9. *Transition:* Transition should include measurable postsecondary goals based on appropriate transition assessments related to training, education, employment, and independent living skills (if needed) for a child beginning at age 16. In addition, transition services needed to assist the child in reaching the goals should be specified. Each child also has to be informed at least one year before reaching the age of majority that his or her rights in special education will transfer to him or her.

   Carlos had one goal related to transition that related to functional reading skills. A statement that his course of study would include courses in the auto body program and the work study program would also be added.

Each IEP must be reviewed and revised annually. The IDEA also provides for amending an IEP without holding a formal IEP meeting (with written parental agreement). Other factors that must be considered when developing the IEP are listed in Figure 1.7.

1. Strengths of the child
2. Concerns of the parents for enhancing the education of their child
3. Results of the initial evaluation or most recent evaluation of the child
4. Academic, developmental, and functional needs of the child
5. Positive behavioral interventions, strategies, and supports to address the child's behavior (i.e., a behavioral intervention plan) in cases where the behavior impedes the child's learning or that of others
6. Language needs of the child if the child is limited English proficient (LEP)
7. Whether to provide Braille instruction if the child is blind or visually impaired
8. Communication needs of the child, especially if the child is deaf or hard of hearing

Note: Regular education teacher of the child shall, to the extent appropriate, participate in the development of the IEP of the child, including the determination of appropriate positive behavioral interventions and supports, and other strategies, and the determination of supplementary aids and services, program modifications, and support for school personnel.

FIGURE 1.7   Factors to Consider in Developing the IEP

Least Restrictive Environment

The principle of *least restrictive environment* (LRE) means that to the maximum extent appropriate, children with disabilities should be educated with children who are nondisabled. This principle is embedded in each IEP and placement decision and includes both academic and nonacademic settings and extracurricular activities like meals and recess. The IDEA also addresses the concept of a *continuum of alternative placements* whereby each school district must maintain a continuum that includes various alternative placements (e.g., instruction in regular education classes, special classes, and special schools). Children must also be educated in their home schools unless the IEP states otherwise.

Essentially, the IEP team is called on to balance the individual's constitutional rights to equal educational opportunity with freedom to associate with one's peers. IEP teams make case-by-case determinations about the extent to which a child might benefit from integration in the regular classroom. For example, LRE for one child might mean education in a private day treatment facility where contact with nondisabled children is minimal. For another child, LRE might mean placement in the regular classroom with accommodations and support from the special education teacher within the regular classroom, where the child is fully integrated with nondisabled peers for the majority of the school day. Figure 1.8 provides the reader with general principles of least restrictive environment, along with self-assessment questions to determine whether the principle is being met. These principles and self-assessments are based on the IDEA, case law, and best practice.

Principle 1

Placement decisions should include consideration of regular education with supplemental aids and services.

Self-Assessment
1. Can education in the regular classroom with supplementary aids and services be achieved satisfactorily?
   Discussion on this might include expectations in the regular classroom and the student's ability to meet those expectations with or without accommodations. If the answer is no, then:
2. Has the district mainstreamed the student to the maximum extent appropriate?
3. Have steps been taken to accommodate the student in the regular class? If no steps have been attempted, that is a matter of concern. In addition, steps should be more than token steps.
4. Is there benefit to the student with a disability in the regular class?
   The discussion might focus on the nature and the severity of the disability and the curriculum of the regular class. The team should look beyond academic benefit.
5. What might be the effect of the student with a disability on other students in the classroom?
   Considerations would include whether the student is likely to monopolize the teacher's time or to disrupt other students.

Principle 2

Decisions should be made in the child's best interest (i.e., most appropriate) and should always be individualized.

Self-Assessment
1. What are the child's special needs as stated in the most recent evaluation?
2. As a teacher, what goals do I think will address these special needs? What do I think the child can accomplish in one year?
3. What supplementary aids, classroom services, and/or related services are needed to carry out these goals?
4. Have I clearly stated my opinion in regard to the above questions in the IEP meeting?

Principle 3

At a minimum, make sure that the regular education teacher who will have a child with a disability in his or her class is fully aware of the nature and extent of the child's IEP.

FIGURE 1.8 Principles of Least Restrictive Environment (LRE)

(continued)

Self-Assessment
1. Has the regular education teacher been invited to the IEP meeting? Regular education teachers should fully participate in the development of the child's IEP.
2. If the regular teacher is unable to attend, have I provided him or her with a copy of the child's IEP?
3. Have I scheduled time to talk to the regular teacher to discuss the IEP?
4. Do I have a mechanism to ensure ongoing support and consultation for the regular teacher?

Principle 4

A full continuum of services should be available.

Self- Assessment
1. As a special education teacher, am I suggesting a particular configuration of services for a child because of my current caseload or existing schedule?
   For example, am I suggesting that a child receive 45 minutes of reading because I schedule that amount of time for reading? Time scheduled for services should be based on time needed to implement goals, not on convenience.
2. Am I willing to be flexible in scheduling and delivery of services?
3. Can I identify one different and appropriate manner of delivering services outside of my current structure?
4. Is the service that I am suggesting for a child based on the child's individual needs and goals?

Principle 5

Document placements that were considered, the rationales for rejection of placements, and the rationale for the recommended placement on the IEP.

Self-Assessment
1. What placements were considered for the child?
2. What precludes the child from placement in a regular class or facility?
3. Why can't supplementary aids and services be used to educate the student in the regular class?
4. For placements considered and rejected, why were the placements rejected?

Note: Failing to clearly indicate on the IEP why a child cannot be educated in the regular classroom is a common violation of the IDEA. If you can't answer the self-assessment questions, think twice about removing the child from the regular classroom!

FIGURE 1.8 *Continued*

Due Process

Due process, the fifth principle, ensures that the child's and parents' rights are safeguarded. Parents are afforded many rights regarding the identification, evaluation, and placement of their child who has or may have a disability. For example, parents must be notified of and provide informed consent for an initial evaluation of the child and initial placement of the child in special education. If parents (or school district personnel) disagree with one another, the IDEA provides for a formal set of proceedings to resolve the conflict, including a resolution meeting, opportunity to meet with a disinterested party, voluntary mediation, and a formal due process hearing. If the conflict is resolved using one of these methods, it is documented in writing and legally binding. Due process procedures from the IDEA are outlined in Figure 1.9, and important details from the dispute resolution process are listed in Figure 1.10.

Parent Participation

The sixth principle, *parent participation*, means that parents have the right to meaningful participation in all decisions made with regard to their child's education. There is nothing like these rights in the rest of our public school system. These rights include, in part, the following:

* Opportunity to examine the child's school records
* The right to notification and participation in meetings about the child
* The right to an independent evaluation
* The right to give or withhold informed consent before the child is evaluated and before initial special education placement

The intent of parent participation is to involve the parents early and often as full partners in the education of the child with a disability.

Right to Educational Achievement

Along with the right to FAPE, children with disabilities have a *right to educational achievement*, the seventh IDEA principle. Having high expectations for children with disabilities and ensuring access to the general education curriculum in the regular education environment is emphasized. States must establish goals for the performance of children with disabilities that are consistent with the goals for all children. Children with disabilities must be included in the general state and districtwide assessment programs, with appropriate accommodations and alternate assessments where necessary to evaluate progress toward these goals. In addition, schools are held responsible for the achievement of all students, including students with disabilities. The IDEA states that special education teachers must be

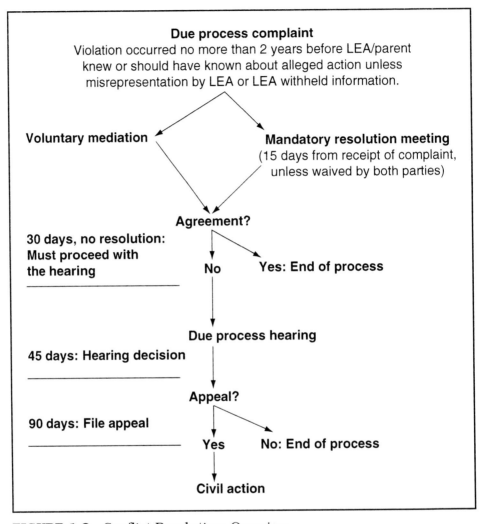

FIGURE 1.9 Conflict Resolution: Overview

"appropriately and adequately prepared" and encourages the use of research-based practices in instruction.

No Child Left Behind Act (NCLB)

In 2001, President George W. Bush signed the reauthorization of the Elementary and Secondary Education Act. Originally enacted in 1965, the purpose was to improve achievement for poor and disadvantaged students. The law also regulates most federal education programs for kindergarten

Mediation Procedures

1. General:
   - Is voluntary
   - Cannot be used to delay due process
   - Conducted by qualified mediator
2. LEA may have procedures for someone who doesn't choose mediation:
   - Opportunity to meet with a disinterested party
   - Explain benefits of and encourage mediation
3. Agreement must be signed by both parties.
4. Agreement is legally binding.
5. Discussions are confidential.

Due Process Complaint

1. Written complaint must be filed with other party, with a copy to the State Education Agency.
2. Complaint content:
   - Child's name
   - Child's address
   - School name
   - Description of nature of problem, including facts
   - Proposed resolution
3. No hearing unless complaint is filed and meets requirements. If complaint is not sufficient, can notify hearing officer within 15 days of receipt; hearing officer determines within 5 days whether complaint is sufficient.
4. If not already done, LEA must send written notice to parent regarding subject matter in complaint within 10 days of receipt of due process complaint. Must include:
   - Why LEA proposed or refused to take action on concern raised in complaint
   - Other options IEP team considered and why those options were rejected
   - Description of evaluation procedure, assessment, or records or report that LEA used as basis for the proposed or refused action
   - Other factors relevant

Note: Except above, party receiving due process complaint must (within 10 days of receipt) send other party a response that addresses issues raised in the complaint.

Resolution Process

1. LEA must hold a resolution meeting within 15 days of complaint receipt.
2. Resolution meeting includes relevant members of IEP team:
   - LEA representation with decision-making authority
   - No attorney for LEA unless parent has an attorney

FIGURE 1.10   Conflict Resolution: Procedure

(continued)

3. Purpose of meeting is to discuss complaint and facts, and to try to resolve the complaint.
4. Meeting may be waived if parent and LEA agree or if mediation occurs.
5. Timelines: If no resolution within 30 days of complaint receipt, due process hearing must occur.
6. If parent fails to participate, timelines are delayed.
7. Agreement:
   • Must be in writing
   • Must be signed by both parties
   • Is legally binding
   • May be voided by either party within 3 business days

FIGURE 1.10 *Continued*

through grade 12. Like all federal laws, it is reviewed and reauthorized by Congress every 5 years and then funds are appropriated to carry it out. In addition, because statutes are usually general, the Department of Education issues regulations and nonregulatory guidance to assist states in carrying out the law. The 2001 revision, No Child Left Behind (NCLB), mandated sweeping changes to public schools and dramatically increased the federal government's involvement in public schools. The goals of the NCLB Act included the following:

* All students will reach high standards, attaining at least proficiency in reading and mathematics (by 2014).
* All students will be able to read by the end of the 3rd grade (by 2014).
* All limited English proficient (LEP) students will be proficient in English.
* All students will be taught by highly qualified teachers (by 2006).
* All students will be educated in learning environments that are safe and drug free.
* All students will graduate from high school.

Five principles formed the foundation of the NCLB Act: accountability to demonstrate that students were meeting outcomes, increased parental choice, school district flexibility and local control, emphasis on research-based teaching methods, and provisions for highly qualified teachers and paraprofessionals. These general principles are reviewed next.

Accountability

All states were mandated to implement a system of statewide *accountability* by setting state standards in reading and mathematics; by assessing all students annually in grades 3, 4, 5, 6, 7, and 8 and once more in grade 10, 11, or 12 on progress toward the standards; and by releasing assessment results to the public. The following steps illustrate how the system was implemented:

1. Each state developed academic standards for all children in reading, mathematics, and science with the mandate that all children will show proficiency by 2014.
2. The state developed tests to assess academic standards annually in grades 3, 4, 5, 6, 7, and 8 and once again in grade 10, 11, or 12.
3. Each state set proficiency standards that schools must attain each year (i.e., adequate yearly progress, or AYP). Again, the mandate was that all children would reach proficiency by the year 2014.
4. The state administered tests to all children (including children with disabilities). It was expected that 95% of children with disabilities would participate in the tests, with or without accommodations. The positive scores of up to 1% of students tested—presumably those with serious cognitive impairments, who are assessed using alternative assessments against alternate achievement standards—could be counted in the calculation of AYP as "proficient." This 1% cap could be increased by special request by either the U.S. Department of Education or the state. If more than 1% of students took the alternate assessment, their proficient scores would not be counted toward meeting AYP goals.
5. Results of the assessments had to be made public, for each school building and by subgroup (i.e., economic disadvantaged, disabled, limited English proficient, and race/ethnicity).
6. For the total group and each subgroup, one question was asked: Did the group meet the progress standard set? If not, sanctions were applied. These sanctions increased in intensity each year of failing to meet AYP goals, and could include reconstituting the school.

As an example, one elementary school, serving children in kindergarten through grade 8, assessed all children in reading and mathematics from grade 3 through grade 8. The school included 45 children with disabilities in the 3rd grade. Of these children, 41 took the standard assessment with some modifications, including extended time and reading the test aloud (except the reading test). Four children took an alternate test, a portfolio, because they were identified as having significant cognitive disabilities and worked toward functional and life skills. All test results, including those from the portfolio, were summarized and made public in a "report card." On the report card, different subgroups,(e.g., students with disabilities) were disaggregated. (Although the subgroup is included as part of the total group scores, the subgroup is also separated from the total group and analyzed.) The report card indicated that the school did not meet adequate yearly progress (AYP) because students with disabilities did not meet AYP. This subgroup prevented the entire school from meeting AYP. After 3 years of not meeting AYP goals, the school had to provide supplemental tutoring for all students.

Increased Parental Choice

If the school (or subgroup) did not meet AYP goals, the school was labeled as low performing. *Increased parental choice* for students in low performing schools included allowing parents to send their student to a better performing public school within the district (not making AYP for 2 consecutive years) and choosing supplemental education services, such as after-school instruction or tutoring (not making AYP for 3 consecutive years). In addition, parents could transfer their student to a safe school within the district if the school of attendance was unsafe or if the student was a victim of a violent crime at school.

To illustrate parental choice, consider Thompson Elementary School, a large school of 800 students in an urban school district. For 3 years, Thompson Elementary did not meet AYP in the area of reading at the 3rd, 4th-, 5th-, and 6th-grade levels. Approximately 100 of the students received special education services and approximately 400 students were eligible for Title I services. Thompson Elementary did not meet AYP because of the reading test results for the entire school as well as for two subgroups: students with disabilities and students from low-income families. In the fourth year, Thompson Elementary was required to offer supplemental educational services outside of the school day to the lowest achieving students in reading. It was decided by school district personnel that students who were at least 2 years below grade level in reading were eligible for these services, and the school district contracted with a private for-profit company approved by the state to provide after-school tutoring in reading. Most of the students with disabilities (85 out of 100) met the criteria of low performance in reading (i.e., 2 years below grade level in reading), and therefore students with disabilities were eligible for the after-school service. The service for these children could not be funded with special education funds, but were paid for by Title I funds. The challenge for the school district was to make sure the private company provided services that were consistent with each child's IEP and that the company had knowledge of the IEP content.

School District Flexibility and Local Control

The next NCLB principle is *school district flexibility and local control,* whereby local school districts (and states) have greater flexibility to transfer funds from one federal grant to another without gaining federal approval. States and school districts could transfer up to 50% of funding received under four major state grant programs (Teacher Quality State Grants, Educational Technology, Innovative Programs, Safe and Drug-Free Schools) to any one of the programs or to Title I without federal government approval. Also, if a district met AYP goals, there would be more freedom to spend Title I funds.

The philosophy behind this principle is similar to the idea of *site-based management*, when a school is allocated funds to use for the purchase of supplies, personnel, and equipment without bureaucratic restrictions because the local school personnel know best what is needed. Similarly, local school districts (and states) know best where to use federal monies to meet local needs.

Research-Based Teaching Methods

The NCLB Act puts a greater emphasis on funding grants for *research-based teaching methods*—teaching practices that have been proven by scientific research to be successful. The act identified five essential components of reading instruction that were based on a review of reading research: phonemic awareness, phonics, vocabulary development, reading fluency, and reading comprehension. In the Reading First State Grant program, for example, the NCLB Act made grants to states (who made the grants available to local school districts on a competitive basis) to use research-based instructional strategies in the area of reading. School districts who were awarded grants had to focus on the essential components of reading instruction for kindergarten through grade 3 teachers and kindergarten through grade 12 special education teachers, preservice coursework for kindergarten through grade 3 teachers, and improving state certification standards. These grants required the use of appropriate and valid reliable assessments used to monitor progress and for diagnostic purposes.

Highly Qualified Teachers and Paraprofessionals

A major principle of the NCLB Act was the emphasis on having *highly qualified teachers and paraprofessionals* in the classroom. In fact, all teachers had to be highly qualified by the 2005–2006 school year. The provisions to become highly qualified were very specific and included the following:

- Teachers must hold a bachelor's degree from a college or university.
- Teachers must have state teacher certification or licensure in the area in which they teach.

* Teachers must demonstrate subject matter competency in each core subject they teach (e.g., English, reading, mathematics, science, foreign language, civics, government, economics, the arts, history, and geography). Passing a state test in each core subject could verify subject matter competence.

These provisions held true for special education teachers if they taught one or more core subject areas to students with disabilities. If the special education teacher successfully completed the state's high objective uniform state standard of evaluation (HOUSSE) addressing the core areas taught, the teacher was considered highly qualified.

Similarly, paraprofessionals who were funded by NCLB money or who worked in a "Title I schoolwide" program site where they provided tutoring, assisted with classroom management or computer instruction, worked with parents, provided support in a library, worked as a translator, or provided support services under the direct supervision of a teacher must be highly qualified. This meant that the paraprofessional had to complete 2 years of study at a college or university or obtain an associate's degree or higher. Without a degree, the paraprofessional could become highly qualified by passing a state or local test in reading, writing, and mathematics.

Junction: IDEA and NCLB

The Individuals with Disabilities Education Improvement Act of 2004 (IDEA) contained at least 60 references to the No Child Left Behind Act (NCLB). Included, in part, were references to the inclusion of students with disabilities in state and district assessment, goals for the performance of all children, the flexible use of IDEA funds to carry out schoolwide programs under the NCLB Act, and assurance that all personnel under the IDEA were appropriately prepared, subject to the provisions in the NCLB Act under "highly qualified" teachers and paraprofessionals. Clearly, the philosophies of the two laws suggested that general education and special education no longer operated as separate systems. The lines between special education and general education continued to fade as all educators assumed responsibility for the education of all children in the public schools.

Since the mid-1980s, the focus of school reform shifted from inputs into the public school system (i.e., resources) to outcomes or outputs (e.g., improvement of learning, students meeting outcomes). In addition, the focus shifted to improvement for *all* students, including students from minority groups, students with disabilities, and students whose primary language was not English. Students with disabilities were no longer left out of the reform movement, but were part of the effort to improve results for all students.

Selected Resources

Statutes

No Child Left Behind, P.L. 107–110 (*http://www.ed.gov/policy/elsec/leg/ esea02/index.html*).

Individuals with Disabilities Education Improvement Act, P.L. 108–446 (*http://edworkforce.house.gov/issues/108th/education/idea/ conferencereport/confrept.htm*).

Regulations

Title I: Improving the Academic Achievement of the Disadvantaged (*http:// www.ed.gov/legislation/FedRegister/finrule/2003–4/120903a.html*).

General

Bush, G. W. (2004, December 3). *President's remarks at the signing of H.R. 1350: Individuals with Disabilities Education Improvement Act of 2004*. Retrieved from the White House Web site (*http://www. whitehouse.gov/news/releases/2004/12/20041203-6.html*).

Council for Exceptional Children. *The new IDEA: CEC's summary of significant issues* (*http://www.cec.sped.org/AM/Template.cfm? Section=Home&TEMPLATE=/CM/ContentDisplay.cfm&CONTENTID= 2552*).

NASDSE: National Association of State Directors of Special Education (*www.nasdse.org*).

NASDSE's IDEA Partnership (*www.ideapartnership.org*).

National Center for Learning Disabilities (*http://www.ncld.org/NCLB*).

NCLB: *Alternate achievement standards for students with the most signifi- cant cognitive disabilities: Non-regulatory guidance*, August 2005 (*http://www.ed.gov/policy/elsec/guid/altguidance.pdf*).

NCLB: *Highly qualified teachers: Revised Title II, Part A: Non-regulatory guid- ance*, August 3, 2005 (*http://www.ed.gov/programs/teacherqual/ guidance.pdf*).

NCLB: *Flexibility for states raising achievement for students with disabilities* (*http://www.ed.gov/policy/elsec/guid/raising/disab-factsheet.pdf*).

U.S. Department of Education. Web site on NCLB (*http://www.ed.gov/ nclb/landing.jhtml*).

U.S. Department of Education. *No Child Left Behind: A desktop reference 2002* (*www.ed.gov/admins/lead/account/nclbreference/ reference.pdf*).

Yell, M. L., & Drasgow, E. (2005). *No child left behind: A guide for profes- sionals*. Upper Saddle River, NJ: Merrill/Prentice Hall.

Chapter **2**

Accountability

CASE 2.1 Brandon

Major issue: Individualized education program (IEP)
Secondary issue: Free appropriate public education (FAPE)

Characters

Tameka Brown, parent
Brandon Brown, 5th-grade child with a disability
Linda Wilson, parent advocate
Patrick Corradini, special education teacher
Kathy Crider, regular education teacher
Monica Hess, special education administrator
Ron Sultan, principal

It was May and the school year was almost finished at Rosemont Elementary School. Tameka Brown, parent of Brandon, and a child advocate, Linda Wilson, walked into the IEP meeting together. Tameka had experience with special education because her mother was a special education teacher in the neighboring school district. Usually Tameka's mother attended each IEP meeting with Tameka, but this time Tameka had requested representation by a child advocate. Tameka was concerned that Brandon would not receive all needed services on his IEP for the next school year. For example, in January, 6 months into the school year, she had discovered that the teacher was not consistently using the FM unit required for Brandon's central auditory processing disorder. These concerns were addressed in an IEP meeting and the teacher now used the FM unit consistently.

The IEP team assembled in the school conference room. Around the table were the following persons: Mr. Corradini, Brandon's special education teacher; Ms. Crider, Brandon's 5th-grade teacher; Ms. Hess, special education administrator; and Mr. Sultan, principal. Ms. Hess began the meeting by introducing participants and then saying, "The purpose of our meeting today is to review Brandon's IEP and his progress. We will also draft a new IEP for next year. Mr. Corradini, will you begin by summarizing Brandon's progress this year?"

Mr. Corradini said, "Yes. As you know, Brandon has made excellent progress this year. I'm so proud of him! He is getting along well with all of the other children in our classroom and seems very happy. I will review each of his goals and talk about his progress for each goal."

Mr. Corradini began to read each goal and discuss progress in each area. He said that Brandon was able to write a complete six-word sentence, and a three-paragraph essay with a beginning, middle, and end. He also said that Brandon was able to follow three-step directions with two prompts while using his FM unit. He also did a better job writing assignments in his daily planner. He concluded by saying, "Brandon has clearly met all of his goals."

As Mr. Corradini talked, Ms. Wilson listened and took notes on a legal pad. She said, "Mr. Corradini, you just reviewed Brandon's goals and stated that he met all of his goals. I'd like to look again at each goal. The first one reads: 'Brandon will write a three-paragraph essay using at least six-word sentences and the essay will be structured to have a beginning, middle, and end.' The goal was to be evaluated weekly based on observations at 91 to 100% accuracy. Now, exactly how do you know he met this goal?"

Mr. Corradini answered, "Well, we write an essay every week in class and I thought back over the last 10 weeks and Brandon followed the paragraph structure about 95% of the time."

Ms. Wilson questioned him further by asking, "Do you have the essays to show that he met the goal at 95% accuracy?"

Mr. Corradini said, "I don't normally keep all of that stuff. I do grade the essays and Brandon was mostly earning B's on them during the last quarter. This clearly shows that he met the goal."

Ms. Wilson shook her head in disbelief, and then continued, "The next goal reads: 'Brandon will follow oral instructions with three steps with two prompts while using his FM unit.' This goal was monitored weekly by observation at 91 to 100% accuracy. Again, Mr. Corradini, how do you know that Brandon met this goal?"

Mr. Corradini said, "It is my professional judgment based on daily observations that Brandon met this goal."

Ms. Wilson went on to say, "The final goal states: 'Brandon will write assignments in a daily planner.' This was to be evaluated weekly, again based on observation at 71 to 80% accuracy. How do you know Brandon met this goal?"

Mr. Corradini began to squirm as he said, "As I reflect on the last 10 weeks, I can say that Brandon wrote seven or eight assignments every day when I checked him out at the end of the day. Again, Brandon's grades improved over the last 10 weeks and if he didn't write his assignments, he couldn't have made those grades."

Ms. Wilson stated, "Mr. Corradini, I would like to see your data. I don't know how you can say that Brandon met these goals with no data to track his progress."

Mr. Corradini answered, "And I told you, Ms. Wilson, Brandon's grades reflect his progress. I don't need to track every goal every day to know that he met his goals. My professional judgment should be enough. If you want to look at data, let's review Brandon's achievement test scores. Brandon was administered the Peabody Individual Achievement Test one year ago. His grade equivalent in reading was 3.2. This spring I administered the same test to him and his grade equivalent in reading was 3.8. This means he made 6 months of progress."

Ms. Wilson asked, "How did Brandon perform on the state test in reading and mathematics?"

Mr. Corradini answered, "He did not meet standards in reading. In fact he was categorized as 'deficient' in reading. In mathematics, Brandon met the standards."

Ms. Wilson responded, "Mr. Corradini, Brandon obviously is not making adequate progress. I simply don't see how 6 months of progress in reading, if it really is 6 months, connects to Brandon's goals. I can see that you do not have data to support your observations. Therefore, I don't think we know if Brandon met his goals. I would even suggest that Brandon is being denied a free appropriate public education because you are not taking responsibility for tracking Brandon's progress. Schools are accountable for each student's progress."

Legal Issues

1. To what extent did Mr. Corradini, the special education teacher, specify how Brandon's progress toward annual goals would be measured and when reports on his progress would be made? Why was this a legal problem?

2. To what extent did Brandon's progress on the state test address his progress toward IEP goals?

Other Issues

1. To what extent is it acceptable to use grades as an assessment of progress toward IEP goals? To what extent is it acceptable to use a general standardized achievement test as an assessment toward IEP goals?

2. How could this potential conflict be resolved?

Activity

Take each goal stated for Brandon in the case and do the following:

1. Rewrite the goal to make it measurable, if needed.
2. Indicate the assessment to be used to track Brandon's progress on the goal.
3. State when and how periodic reports will be made on Brandon's progress for the parent.

CASE 2.2   Sonya

Major issue: State assessment

Secondary issue: Free appropriate public education (FAPE)

Character

Sonya Brown, high school special education teacher

Sonya Brown:

I'm a little confused about who is supposed to take the state test. Last year, our district administrator decided that all 100 students in special education would take the *state test*. This year, he decided that 70 of the 100 students in special education would take the *alternate state test*, which is a portfolio. In our state, there must be at least 40 students in special education taking the state test to count the scores as a subgroup. In our case, there will no longer be a subgroup for special education and their scores won't be summarized and count as a subgroup. This probably will help the school meet adequate yearly progress (AYP). If just one subgroup does not meet AYP, the entire school is sanctioned.

The state test results for students in special education were the reason my school did not meet AYP. I have been here 15 years as a special education math teacher and this is the most pressure I have ever felt. When our principal, Mr. Wheeler, called the faculty together to review the state test results 2 weeks ago, I think we were somewhat surprised at the results. At the faculty meeting, we reviewed our school report card and the summary table was quite clear.

By the end of our meeting, other faculty members were very upset with the results and even made remarks to the special education teachers that we must make changes or the whole school would suffer.

As I said, I have been a special education teacher for 15 years and I really believe that we can raise test scores. For example, I teach special education math. My classes mostly consist of students with learning disabilities, behavior disorders, and mild mental retardation. Many of our 100 students in special education take the special education math class. In fact, most of our students with disabilities take the majority of their classes in the special education program. I teach the same content as the regular education teacher in math and we use the same textbook. However, by November or December of each year, I find that my students are simply unable to understand the content. So I deviate from

	Percent Tested on State Test: Reading	Percent Tested on State Test: Mathematics	Percent Meeting/ Exceeding Standards: Reading	Percent Meeting/ Exceeding Standards: Mathematics	Graduation Rate
State AYP minimum target	95.0%	95.0%	40.0%	40.0%	66.0%
All students	99.0% (Yes)*	99.0% (Yes)*	50.7% (Yes)*	41.2% (Yes)*	100.0% (Yes)*
Disabled	100.0% (Yes)*	100.0% (Yes)*	10.5% (No)*	1.8% (No)*	100.0% (Yes)*
Economic disadvantaged	98.0% (Yes)*	98.0% (Yes)*	37.5% (Yes)*	37.0% (Yes)*	100.0% (Yes)*

Note: To meet AYP in this state, these conditions are required: (1) At least 95% tested for reading and mathematics and for all groups and subgroups; (2) At least 40% meet/exceed standards for all groups and at least 37% for all subgroups to compensate for error in measurement for smaller subgroup sizes or meet Safe Harbor requirements. Safe Harbor: Subgroups with fewer than 40 students are not reported. Safe Harbor only applies to subgroups. In order for Safe Harbor to apply, a subgroup must decrease by 10% the percentage of scores that did not meet standards from the previous year plus meet the graduation rate for the subgroup. Safe Harbor allows the school an alternate method to meet subgroup minimum targets on achievement.

*Did group/subgroup meet AYP?

the general education curriculum to teach math that is more functional, or I take longer to present the same concept. I try to help the students make progress toward their IEP goals and the general education curriculum goals. One of the problems is that the IEP goals and general education curriculum goals aren't always the same. This is because the students in special education function at a much lower level than students in regular education. One of my colleagues teaches a second section of math in the special education classroom. He doesn't use the general education textbook at all. He creates the curriculum depending upon who is in his classroom. In fact, he told me that students receive "packets" of worksheets that are on various levels and he tells students how many worksheets they must complete for the day. Students then work at their own pace to complete the day's work and ask questions when they don't understand something. Some students are working on basic computation, others are working on prealgebra, and others are working on geometry. I think this works for the other teacher. I don't really see a problem with this method as long as the students are progressing. We don't have to use the same texts or methods. Our students are in special education, aren't they? We are supposed to individualize programs, aren't we? I try to maintain the connection to the general education curriculum in math as long as possible each year and the other special education teacher doesn't—so what?

Wow! It was just a matter of time before our entire school faced serious sanctions because I seriously doubt that students in special education can ever meet or exceed state standards. The students in special education just function at a lower level. Maybe the administrator is thinking is that we will have a better chance of meeting AYP if our students take the alternate assessment. However, I wonder about the students' IEPs. We already conducted annual reviews and indicated for each student his or her participation in the state testing system. If the district administrator follows through on the decision to have most students take the alternate assessment and most IEPs indicate that the students will take the state test, are we really following the IEPs? What will happen?

Legal Issues

1. Interpret the state test results for students with and without disabilities in this case. Also, describe Safe Harbor and how it applies to this case.

2. What are the possible consequences of the administrator's decision to require that the majority of students in special education take an alternate test rather than the regular state test? Consider both IDEA and NCLB.

Other Issues

1. Why do you think the district administrator decided that the majority of students with disabilities would take the alternate state test (i.e., portfolio)?

2. Who is accountable for the progress of the students in special education discussed in this case?

Activity

Why are students in special education unable to meet state standards in this case? List some possible reasons and discuss what a school could do to help students in special education meet state standards.

Chapter **3**

Participation in High-Stakes Assessment

CASE 3.1   Tammy

Major issue: State assessment

Secondary issue: Accommodations

Characters

Tammy Young, 6th-grade student with learning disability

Terri Mossman, Tammy's mother

Mark Richards, principal

Roberta Smith, superintendent

Outside of the Central Office, the reporter asked, "Dr. Smith, you recently gave an award to Mr. Richards for raising test scores at Slay Elementary School. Don't you feel the award should be taken away and Mr. Richards disciplined for purposely excluding students in special education from the state test?"

Dr. Smith looked directly at the newspaper reporter as she stated angrily, "I don't have to give you information about a principal in my district."

"But Dr. Smith," the reporter asked, "Did Mr. Richards deserve the award?"

Again, Dr. Smith stated angrily, "Do you deserve every award you receive? Of course he didn't deserve it. But I will not talk about disciplining a school employee to a newspaper reporter!" After that comment, Dr. Smith walked into the Central Office.

The whole community was talking about what happened at Slay Elementary School. No Child Left Behind permitted a very small percentage of students with significant disabilities to take an alternate

Slay Elementary School

	Percent Tested on State Reading Test		Percent Meeting/Exceeding Standards on State Reading Test	
	Percent	Met AYP?	Percent	Met AYP?
State AYP minimum target	95%	Not applicable	40%	Not applicable
All students in this school	97% (*98%)	Yes (*Yes)	43% (*20%)	Yes (*No)
Students with disabilities in this school	30% (*99%)	No (*Yes)	Not reported (if fewer than 45 students) (*8%)	Not reported (if fewer than 45 students) (*No)

Note: To meet AYP, at least 95% of students must be tested in reading for the total group ("All students") and subgroups (e.g., students with disabilities). In addition, 37% of each subgroup must meet/exceed state standards in reading. Fewer than 45 students in a subgroup are not reported and not counted.
*Previous year results.

assessment instead of the state assessment to track students' progress toward state standards. One year earlier, only 20% of students met or exceeded the state standards in reading at Slay Elementary and 98% of students took the test, including 99% of students with disabilities. This past April, only 30% of students with disabilities took the test, systematically excluding 70% of students in special education. This resulted in dramatic increases in the total number of students meeting state standards. In fact, 43% of Slay Elementary students met or exceeded state standards in reading this year (compared with 20% the previous year). At the other two elementary schools in the district, only 31% of students met or exceeded the state standards in reading. In part, the accompanying table, summarizing data, showed the clear differences with the previous year.

Initially, Mr. Richards was publicly commended for the test score increases and he was given an award from the Board of Education, which was presented by the superintendent at the Board's monthly meeting. Just after the meeting, the newspaper reporter began to review the data on testing and interview parents at Slay Elementary. This resulted in many questions about how the school could make huge test score increases in only 2 years. The data suggested that many special education students had been excluded from participating in the state test. Interviewing Slay Elementary students and their parents, as well as reviewing district documents, confirmed this suspicion.

One student who was not allowed to take the state test was Tammy Young, a 12-year-old Slay Elementary student. Tammy's mother, Terri Mossman, stated in an interview that excluding Tammy from taking the state test kept her from understanding her daughter's academic skill level. She also stated that the exclusion damaged Tammy's self-concept by treating her differently from her peers. Ms. Mossman said that Tammy had struggled for years with feelings of inadequacy because she had a reading disability and was segregated from other children in a special education class. Tammy hated school and often did not try to complete assigned tasks when singled out as different from her peers. The week that the state test was given, Tammy came home very upset and teary-eyed. She said that her name was called over the intercom to go to the special education classroom during the testing periods. She felt like there must have been a reason that she didn't take the test, said Ms. Mossman. Ms. Mossman stated to the reporter, "Everyone else took the test. Why couldn't my daughter take it?"

Meanwhile, the reporter investigated the situation by researching public data on the assessment. It was discovered that No Child Left Behind permitted the exclusion of only the most severely disabled students from taking the standard state test (about 1% of total enrollment). Apparently, this prevented schools from increasing test scores by exempting the lowest test-takers, which usually included students in special education. However, it was likely that this school cheated by excluding a large group of students in special education from taking the test.

A few days after the reporter attempted to talk with Dr. Smith, Dr. Smith held a private conference with Mr. Richards. As Mr. Richards entered the office, Dr. Smith was clearly upset and angry. Dr. Smith stated, "Mark, I was aggressively approached by a reporter at the front door today questioning the school report card data from Slay Elementary. It was alleged that you cheated and did not allow most students in special education to take the state test. Please help me understand what happened. I will need to report to our School Board and I know the press will attend the next meeting."

Mr. Richards hesitated, but said, "Look, Roberta, we've worked together for a long time. You know that we are in a difficult position. I am trying to administer a building of 231 youngsters where 100% are minorities and from low incomes. About 20% are students in special education. The odds are against us in doing well on the state test. I know that many of our students are learning, but I just can't show this when I have to include test scores from students in special education. Their results clearly pull down our scores. I just got tired of this and told my special education teachers that only the highest performing students in special education would take the state test and that the remainder did not have to take any test. I just wanted to present a clear picture of what the majority of students in Slay could do. I didn't think I was doing anything wrong."

At the next School Board meeting, the Board went into executive session to privately discuss personnel matters. When they returned to the open public session, they voted unanimously to remove Mr. Richards from his principalship and place him as a classroom teacher in the 6th grade.

Legal Issues

1. Interpret the table that partially summarizes the state test. What conclusions can you draw?

2. Did the school district follow the law in deciding which students in special education should take the state test? How do you know?

Other Issues

1. Did Mr. Richards cheat on the state test scores even if his motives were honest? What leads you to this conclusion?

2. What role should the special education teacher have taken in this case? Special education administrator?

Activity

Look on your state board of education's Web site and locate the state test results for your school. Review the rate of participation for students with disabilities at one grade level. Then review the results for that grade level. Describe what you learned about your school. What recommendations might you make to improve test scores?

CASE 3.2   Paul

Major issue: State assessment

Secondary issue: Transition

Characters

Shaundra Williams, parent

Paul Williams, high school student with Down syndrome and mild mental impairment

Terrance Brooks, special education teacher

Pam Wright, special education supervisor

The IEP participants sat around the conference table for what should have been a routine annual review. Paul, who would enter 11th grade next year, sat next to his mother, Shaundra Williams. Other school staff members sat around the table. They included Terrance Brooks, Paul's special education teacher, and Pam Wright, special education supervisor.

"Paul has experienced a very successful and productive year," began Mr. Brooks. "He is a hard worker and, although shy, has become more assertive about asking questions when he isn't sure of something. As you know, Paul's program is focused on the development of life skills. We still work on basic academic skills, especially reading and basic math, but we also emphasize the application of these skills in the community. Paul will be eligible and ready for the work-study program next year, and I anticipate that he will be able to work at a local restaurant cleaning tables. We will also continue to make regular trips into the community to develop Paul's communication skills and work weekly on the development of leisure skills. Next year, Paul will have, in addition to the work-study program, a cooking class, math and reading classes, and weekly community integration trips. We will also continue to bowl and swim on Friday afternoons. As you see on his current IEP, Paul has met all of his annual goals. We will continue our focus on the same areas but work on more complex skills, like reading and following a bus schedule to get to the work site. Paul will have a job coach accompany him to his job site."

The team discussed Paul's progress in detail. Paul was reading at a beginning 1st-grade level and could complete math problems at a beginning

2nd-grade level. He had many friends, both disabled and nondisabled. He attended some school-related activities, like home football games, with his family and friends. He was very social and sometimes had to be reminded to attend to the task at hand rather than talk to his friends. Paul's transition plan was discussed and reviewed. Paul's long-term transition goal focused on living semi-independently with a friend in an apartment setting and working within the community in a service occupation. It was anticipated that Paul might need a job coach initially for a new work situation to learn the routine and learn how to complete time sheets and other paperwork. After the initial stages at a work setting, it seemed realistic for Paul to function independently with regular, but not daily, support. The work-study program was one service designed to help Paul become accustomed to a structured work setting in the community. During the past year, Paul held a nonpaying job in the school office and in the school cafeteria, with a job coach present.

Shaundra Williams smiled as Mr. Brooks talked about Paul's progress during the year. She was very pleased with her son's progress and felt that his transition plan was appropriate. Although she was worried about how Paul would function independently when he was an adult, she felt that the school program would help both of them move toward a successful future. Ms. Williams felt that her experience with the school had been positive and she especially liked Paul's current teacher, Mr. Brooks. As a single parent, it was very important to work with the school, because Ms. Williams knew she couldn't do everything alone.

The last section of the IEP dealt with Paul's ability to take the state standardized achievement test, part of which included the scholastic aptitude test. Ms. Wright stated, "As you may know, Ms. Williams, the federal No Child Left Behind Act requires students to be assessed on the state standardized achievement test. Part of this test includes the scholastic aptitude test. Paul has, until high school, been taking the alternate assessment, which is a portfolio. Last year, we allowed too many students with disabilities to take an alternate test. This year, our superintendent has informed me that all students must take the state test, unless the student's disability is severe. Paul has Down syndrome and only a mild mental impairment, so he will have to take the test."

Ms. Williams looked surprised and a lengthy discussion ensued about the content of the test. Ms. Williams stated, "Paul cannot read or understand material at the high school level, much less know the answers! I would love for him to participate, to be normal, but he's not. And to penalize him by making him suffer through this test is crazy!"

Mr. Brooks agreed by saying, "I measure Paul's progress by how he is advancing toward his IEP goals, not on standardized tests. Paul has been taught an alternative curriculum and lacks exposure to the general education curriculum. He would be totally lost on the test. Even modifications like reading the test aloud, using a calculator, or giving him extra time would not help. I'm worried about his self-esteem. Paul is really sensitive about his academic abilities, and I'm afraid that this test would emphasize to him what he is unable to do. Shouldn't we be focusing on what he has learned as a result of his individualized program and how he is making progress on his transition to an independent adulthood?"

Ms. Wright was unpersuaded: "All students must meet the standards upon which the test is based by the 2014–2015 school year, and it is expected that students receiving special education services must also meet the standards."

But Paul's mother continued: "Ms. Wright, if Paul could meet the standards, or even come close, he wouldn't require the type of intensive special education services he receives. I absolutely won't allow him to take the test! If I have to hold him out of school on the test days, I will do so!"

After a heated discussion, Ms. Williams left the IEP meeting feeling very upset. Later that evening, she received a telephone call from Mr. Brooks, who encouraged her to send Paul to school on the day of the test. He emphasized that he would provide encouragement and support for Paul. Reluctantly, Ms. Williams agreed.

On the first day of testing, Paul went to school anticipating the test. When presented with the test, Paul became very upset. He vomited in the restroom and told Mr. Brooks that he was ill. Mr. Brooks, although sympathetic, knew that Paul was having an adverse reaction to the test. He encouraged Paul to try on the test. Although Paul stayed at school that day, he finally just marked any answers on the test and felt humiliated. When he arrived at home later that day, he was in tears.

Legal Issues

1. Under No Child Left Behind, what percentage of students with disabilities must take the state test? Did the school follow the law? How do you know?

2. Who makes the decision, according to IDEA, about the inclusion of a student with a disability taking the state test (with or without accommodations)? Did the school follow the law? How do you know?

Other Issues

1. If the purpose of NCLB is to ensure that all students are meeting state standards in reading and mathematics, how does a transition plan like Paul's fit?

2. How should the administrator handle this situation? The teacher?

Activity

Search your state government's Web site for your state Board of Education and answer the following questions for your school:

1. What percent of students with disabilities are meeting state standards in reading and math?
2. What percent of students without disabilities are meeting state standards in reading and math?
3. Compare the results for both groups.
4. Has your school made adequate yearly progress (AYP)?
5. If either your state or your school did not meet AYP, what is the reason?
6. Share the results with a cohort group of students and compare results.

Chapter **4**

Referral and Prereferral Process

CASE 4.1 Jon

Major issue: Response to intervention
Secondary issue: Eligibility

Characters

   Ms. McKinney, kindergarten teacher
   Jon Lange, kindergarten student
   Ms. Lange, parent
   Ms. Poppy, special education teacher
   Ms. Kola, special education administrator

It was the first meeting in January for the problem-solving team at Richland Elementary School. Ever since the team began working with children 2 years ago, many children had received assistance outside of special education. In fact, the team was so successful that it was used as a model for other districts The team consisted of two elementary teachers (one primary and one intermediate), the school psychologist, and the special education teacher. The intent was to provide research-based interventions for children experiencing difficulties achieving in school. One tool used by the team included the Dynamic Indicators of Basic Early Literacy Skills (DIBELS). This was used to assess early elementary children's reading skills and to track progress for children receiving special interventions. At this meeting, the case of Jon Lange, a kindergarten student, was to be discussed. It was early January and Jon was experiencing difficulty with reading readiness skills.

Jon and his mother had moved to the district at the beginning of the school year. Ms. Lange said that Jon had never attended preschool and that the family moved from a rural farm community to the new district.

Jon did not have siblings and his father often was away from home for several weeks at a time driving a truck. Jon's mother worked part-time as a waitress. While at work, Ms. Lange arranged for a neighbor to care for Jon. Ms. Lange said the family had little money for books or magazines and that she was often too tired to read aloud to Jon. She was very happy that the new school district took an interest in Jon's learning. She really wanted Jon to graduate from high school, something neither she nor her husband had accomplished. Early in the school year, Jon's DIBELS scores indicated that he was at risk in prereading skills. At the time, Ms. McKinney, Jon's teacher, thought the scores might reflect the fact that Jon did not come to school with previous prereading experience. However, the current assessment results indicated that he continued to experience difficulty, and Ms. McKinney asked for assistance from the problem-solving team. Ms. Lange was again grateful for the help from the team. The following recent scores were obtained for Jon on DIBELS:

Initial Sounds Fluency: 4 (Deficient)

Letter Naming Fluency: 17 (Some Risk)

Phonemic Segmentation Fluency: 6 (At Risk)

Nonsense Word Fluency: 3 (At Risk)

The team first reviewed Jon's current assessment results and discussed how Jon was progressing in kindergarten. Ms. McKinney stated that although Jon was now demonstrating age-appropriate math skills and social skills, his prereading skills were deficient. The team decided to target phonemic awareness and letter naming for improvement. The intervention consisted of using a special program focusing on the phonemic awareness. Ms. McKinney and her educational assistant would use direct teaching to implement the program for 30 minutes per day. In addition, Jon would participate in a special reading program in the library three times a week, where a volunteer would read stories aloud to small groups of children. The special education teacher, Ms. Poppy, would monitor Jon's progress using DIBELS on a weekly basis. The team decided to meet again in 8 weeks.

At the end of 8 weeks, the team reviewed graphs documenting Jon's progress. Although Jon was making some improvement, the team was still concerned about his progress. They decided to add after-school reading tutoring to the intervention. This would supplement the other two interventions by providing small group assistance twice a week in reading. Again, the team decided to meet in 8 weeks.

Eight weeks later, Jon's progress was reviewed. His performance on DIBELS indicated the following scores:

Letter Naming Fluency: 27 (At Risk)

Phonemic Segmentation Fluency: 9 (Deficient)

Nonsense Word Fluency: 11 (At Risk)

In addition, Ms. McKinney shared the kindergarten skill checklist in reading, math, motor skills, and language. Although Jon did not meet the expectations for kindergarten students in reading, he met all skills in math, language, and motor skills. After some discussion, the team determined that Jon might be in need of special education services and they referred him for an evaluation. The referral form was completed by the team and forwarded to Ms. Kola, the special education administrator. Upon receipt by the special education administrator, Ms. Lange was asked to sign written consent for the evaluation.

Three weeks later, after additional information was gathered, the team met to discuss the results of Jon's evaluation. In addition to the data compiled initially, the problem-solving team gathered social developmental and health information and conducted intelligence and achievement testing. Jon's overall intelligence test score was 82, which was within the low average range. His achievement test scores were also within the low average range: reading, 79; mathematics, 85; and written language, 80. There was not a significant discrepancy between Jon's overall ability—that is, IQ—and his achievement test scores. Even though Jon did not demonstrate a significant discrepancy between ability and achievement, the team members agreed that Jon had a learning disability and was in need of special education intervention. The basis for the decision was the lack of response to intervention in the area of reading.

The team drafted an IEP to be implemented at the beginning of the next school year in 1st grade. The IEP included continuance of services implemented in kindergarten, plus a special language-based reading program. This program was to be implemented in the 1st-grade classroom by the special education teacher. The special education teacher would monitor Jon's progress on a regular basis. Ms. Lange was very pleased with the program and also decided to place Jon in a weekly library reading time program at the local public library.

Legal Issues

1. How does the Individuals with Disabilities Education Improvement Act address eligibility for learning disability? Did the LEA follow the law in Jon's case? How do you know?

2. At what point did the team refer Jon for a special education evaluation? Should the district have requested parental consent before administering DIBELS? Why or why not?

Other Issues

1. What was the role of the problem-solving team in this case?

2. Describe how regular education and special education professionals worked together for Jon's benefit in this case. What other joint activities could you suggest?

3. Review the definition of *learning disability* as stated in IDEA. Compare and contrast learning disability eligibility using a discrepancy formula versus response to intervention (as in Jon's case). What are the advantages and disadvantages to implementing each system of learning disability identification?

Activity

Read information about DIBELS at *http://dibels.uoregon.edu.* Describe the purpose of DIBELS and how it could be implemented to assist in the development of research-based interventions with children.

CASE 4.2   James

Major issue: State assessment
Secondary issue: Eligibility

Characters

James Delaney, special education coordinator
Julie Williams, 3rd-grade teacher
Mary Mehachko, 4th-grade teacher
Jill Wright, kindergarten teacher
Ruby Long, 3rd-grade student
Jeff Prince, 4th-grade student
Jake Shelby, kindergarten student
Jane Moss, principal

Julie Williams, 3rd-grade teacher, pulled the memo from her mailbox, read it quickly, and felt immediately upset. How could they do this? A child in her classroom, Ruby Long, would have to wait until next year to be referred and evaluated for special education services. This was so unfair! She reread the memo:

> To: Building Principals and Classroom Teachers
> From: James Delaney, Special Education Coordinator
>
> Date: March 31
> Re: Referrals to Special Education
>
> New referrals for special education evaluations will cease on April 1. After that date, referrals for special education must be held until the beginning of the next school year. We must focus on conducting the 120 reevaluations that are due this school year and it is simply impossible for the school psychologist to squeeze any more evaluations into this school year. There are several students that teachers have expressed concern about this year, but each school will have to deal with these problems as best they can until next year when it will not be so busy. If you have questions or concerns, please don't hesitate to contact me.

As she walked into the teacher's lounge, Julie stated, "Did you read this memo from James Delaney?"

Two other teachers, Mary Mehachko, 4th grade, and Jill Wright, kindergarten, responded together, "Yes!"

Julie continued, "Do you remember the student, Ruby Long, who I mentioned yesterday? She just moved into the district this year from an inner-city school in Illinois. I suspect that she has not received good teaching or instruction. Because of this possibility, I waited to refer her, to see how much progress she would make before I completed the referral forms. However, I feel like I'm always providing extra help and tutoring just for her! She receives Title I reading, but it is simply not enough. She took the state test this year and was in the "Academic Warning" category in both reading and math. Now I'm told that she can't be referred for a special education evaluation. By the time she is referred and evaluated, we will be into October of next year. Look how much time will be lost!"

Mary Mehachko agreed and said, "I know exactly how you feel. I have a similar situation, except that my student, Jeff Prince, has been with me in 4th grade all year. Jeff does well in math and on any oral tasks, but he struggles in reading. I have tried every technique I know and he is still far behind his grade level. Even with Title I reading, he isn't catching up. On the state test, he was in the "Meets" category for math, but in the "Academic Warning" category in reading. He will be almost one third of the way through 5th grade before anyone even evaluates him!"

The third teacher, Jill Wright, said, "Yes, I agree that this isn't fair. I know that both of you are under a great deal of pressure because your students have to take the state test and our school is in the second year of not meeting annual yearly progress. We're all under pressure, but this certainly doesn't help the situation—not being able to secure help for these children. But just wait until you get Jake Shelby in 3rd and 4th grade. I know he's just in kindergarten now, but if he doesn't get help soon, he will be a disaster in a few years. I have worked closely with his mother this year and she has been so supportive. We jointly carried out a point system to help manage and control his behavior. He also has attention deficit hyperactive disorder, but he seems so angry and is sometimes violent. Although our point system has helped, he is far from under control—and if he can't be referred until next school year, I feel sorry for his 1st-grade teacher!"

After this conversation, the three teachers agreed to talk with the principal, Jane Moss. After school, they approached Jane in her office. Each explained the frustration of working with a child who was experiencing difficulty, academically and behaviorally. Although the principal empathized with them, it was out of her control to change the policy of the special education administrator.

However, Jane talked to James Delaney after the next principals' meeting. "James," she began, "I want to talk to you about your memo stating that referrals cannot be made for the remainder of the school year. Several teachers in my building have been working with children who display significant academic and/or behavioral weaknesses. They have delayed making a referral to implement strategies to help these children so that a referral to special education would be a last resort. Now they are very frustrated that they have to wait until next year."

James did not hesitate as he responded, "I know that many needy children exist in the district, Jane. However, try to understand my position. We have only one school psychologist to conduct evaluations and she is swamped with 120 reevaluations that are due this year. I don't have any other choice. You'll just have to do the best you can this year and refer these children at the beginning of next year."

Jane expected this answer, but still felt discouraged. She left wondering how these children would ever succeed in school and how her building would ever meet state standards.

Legal Issues

1. Is it legal to discontinue referrals at an arbitrary point in the school year? How do you know?
2. Is a school psychologist necessary for all evaluations? What are the components and requirements for conducting an evaluation? A reevaluation?

Other Issues

1. How might "response to intervention" and the establishment of a prereferral system help these children?
2. How do the children in this case affect the results on the state test and contribute to AYP for the school?
3. How should this issue be resolved?

Activity

In a small group, discuss how this issue could be resolved legally. Draft a memo to the superintendent of schools to detail your plan of resolving the issue. Include a summary of the problematic issue, the background of the issue, at least two possible solutions (with advantages and disadvantages of each), your recommended solution, and your rationale.

Chapter **5**

Zero Reject, Child Find, and Discipline

CASE 5.1   Brian

Major issue: Discipline
Secondary issue: Eligibility

Characters

Brian Demko, 9th-grade student
Ms. Demko, parent
Mr. Rodgers, high school principal
Mrs. Pullman, English teacher
Mr. Rodriguez, special education supervisor

Mrs. Pullman:

I have been teaching the freshman English class for 10 years. Most of my colleagues don't like to teach this class because some of the students are immature and less than motivated. In addition, there is often a great variance of abilities within each class, from above average skills in reading and writing to low average skills, and it is difficult to meet all students' needs. However, I enjoy teaching freshman English because the students are a challenge. Few of my students receive special education services, so I am the sole provider of reading and writing assistance. My classes average 25 students and I often offer before- and after-school tutoring and sometimes offer extra study time during my planning period for a test.

Just recently, I had an unfortunate altercation with one of my students, Brian. Brian is a very bright student who has exceptional reading and writing skills, but he often barely makes D's in my class. From a review of his records, I discovered that Brian was evaluated for special education services in the 4th grade but was found not eligible for services.

Further, his records revealed a history of D's and F's in many classes. There were no disciplinary records, although from my observations I could tell that Brian seemed to become angry very easily. Sometimes in class when the work became difficult, he would refuse to respond or put his head on his desk pretending to sleep.

One day, I offered to assist Brian in studying and reviewing for an upcoming English test. When he arrived during his study hall, Brian already had experienced a bad day. He said he already spent several class periods in detention. Brian was rude and disrespectful to other students in the classroom who also needed to study for the test. Brian began shouting out answers and insulting other students, which caused an overall disturbance. As his behavior continued to escalate, I asked him to return to the detention room in the office, giving him a referral. At first Brian refused to leave, and then he stormed out of my classroom. He apparently went back to the detention room, where he was later released to attend his last hour computer class. Brian enjoyed working with the computer and enjoyed relative success in this class. During the computer class that day, however, instead of working on his assignment, Brian chose to write a hate letter describing in detail how he was "going to blow up the school and kill all of the teachers who made him come to school to work like hell." Several students were aware that Brian was writing this letter, but said nothing.

The next morning a computer teacher found Brian's letter and immediately contacted the principal. Brian was suspended from school for 10 days pending an expulsion hearing. His mother was contacted by telephone and given a letter of suspension. The police were also contacted and Brian was arrested. Rumor and panic filled the high school and students expressed concern to teachers and administrators. The high school principal sent a letter to parents detailing the events (not using any names) and stating that the student in question was not in attendance at the school.

Ms. Demko:

I am so upset! I can't believe that Brian has done something this stupid! And the school—why didn't they call me before contacting the police? I wonder if Brian is emotionally disturbed and needs help.

Of the three children my husband and I adopted, my biggest worry is Brian. When he was tested in 4th grade for special education, he was not eligible for services. In fact, he tested as extremely bright—intelligence quotient of 130. He is so cute and is a natural athlete—he never engaged in a ball sport where he didn't instantly excel. He is a natural leader among his friends and he mostly hangs out with the same group he's been with since early grade school, which is a mix of professionals' children, working class, white, and diverse races. And yet he's angry all the time. I know our adoption of Brian and two siblings, a sister and brother, was difficult for all of them. The children were mixed race, had different fathers, and had been severely neglected when they came to live with my husband and me.

Last year, Brian decided to see how close he could get to failing classes and still get promoted to 9th grade—he even told me about this plan! He started out with two F's and D's. By the fourth quarter, he had an F in every academic class. He had 11 F's over the four quarters, and if he had received 13 F's he would have been retained in 8th grade.

He started fires using lacquer thinner in the basement and caught a nearby table on fire. He and his friends almost caught a garage on fire, but no one claimed responsibility. On one occasion, he sneaked out of the house from his second-story window to run around the neighborhood at midnight. He lies about anything, any time. He even steals money from our wallets. My husband and I can't trust him to go where he says he's going or be back on time. I pull the leash tighter and tighter, and he gets angrier and angrier. I let the leash loose sometimes and the next thing I know I'm getting a phone call from the police. The most recent incident was throwing rocks into traffic from a railroad bridge. I could go on and on.

Brian sees a psychiatrist for 10 minutes every 2 months and he takes 40 milligrams of Celexa. I'm not sure it makes any difference. My husband and I attend an adoption support group twice a week and we also get family counseling, but nothing seems to help. One time, Brian threw a wastebasket through the second-story window and wrenched the handrail from the staircase. He has cursed at me, told me he hates me, and raised his fist to hit me—but he always backs down. This time, though, I fear that Brian is in real trouble.

Mr. Rodgers:

I've faced many discipline incidents in my 25 years as principal, but this is the first time I've ever had a student who threatened to kill everyone. I simply will not allow this student into my building again. Now the parents think he has a disability! I don't care if he has one or not—he will not be allowed to attend this school. I have to protect all students and staff in this school. The next step in the disciplinary process is to hold an expulsion hearing, which is scheduled for next week. Brian and his parents will be asked to attend and both sides will present evidence. The hearing officer (our assistant superintendent of schools) will then make a recommendation to the board of education regarding possible expulsion. I think this is a solid case and the evidence speaks for itself. Brian appeared to make a choice to harm others and cannot be allowed back at this school.

Mr. Rodriguez:

I didn't initially know anything about this student, Brian Demko. However, after looking into the situation, I found a special education file! Brian was evaluated in 4th grade for a possible disability. He apparently was adopted along with his two siblings and was having a difficult adjustment. However, the evaluation indicated that Brian was very bright and academically capable. Emotionally, it was stated that he was going through a normal adjustment given his difficult life to that point and his adoption. His adoptive parents were getting help from a support group and the family was receiving counseling. At school, Brian was somewhat disruptive, but always complied after the teacher made some accommodations.

The questions in my mind are: Did the school have knowledge that Brian might be a child with a disability? Was Brian entitled to rights under the Individuals with Disabilities Education Improvement Act? After talking with the principal and teachers, I think Brian is entitled to rights under IDEA. I will suggest that the behavior incident be considered a referral for an expedited evaluation, and then a manifestation determination will be held. First, an IEP team will be convened to gather evaluation information to determine if Brian has a disability. If Brian has a disability, the team will then discuss the following questions to determine whether Brian's behavior is a manifestation of his disability:

* Was his conduct caused by or did it have a direct and substantial relationship to his disability?
* Was Brian's conduct the direct result of the school district's failure to implement the IEP?

It is difficult to determine the outcome of this process, but I know a referral must be made and an expedited evaluation must occur.

Legal Issues

1. Did the school district legally "have knowledge" that Brian might be a child who had a disability? What evidence supports your answer? What factors form the legal basis of knowledge to show that a district "has knowledge" that a child might have a disability?
2. Do the protections of IDEA apply to Brian? How do you know?
3. Can the school district expel Brian? Explain.

Other Issues

1. Do you think Brian has a disability? What is the basis for your decision?
2. Should students without identified disabilities be eligible for protection under IDEA in disciplinary situations? Why or why not?

Activity

Discuss in a small group the specific assessment information that should be collected to determine if Brian has a disability. List the assessments, who will gather the information, and a time line for the completion of the evaluation. You may wish to review the components of an evaluation as specified in IDEA.

CASE 5.2 Terrance

Major issue: Discipline

Secondary issue: Transition

Characters

Terrance Young, 10th-grade student with a learning disability

Karen Young, parent

James Logan, high school principal

Mary Jones, special education administrator

Shondra Hicks, special education teacher

Terrance always experienced difficulty with reading, even though he was not identified as having a learning disability until 6th grade. He had been previously evaluated in 3rd grade, but found not eligible for special education services. It was in 6th grade that he began failing courses. His overall ability indicated an IQ score of 74, with low average verbal skills (standard score 81) and below average performance skills (standard score 63). However, these scores were viewed as low estimates of his abilities. Terrance had age-appropriate listening comprehension skills, weak decoding skills (including poor phonetic abilities), and weak writing skills (including poor sentence construction, spelling, capitalization, punctuation, and handwriting). He had attended the same rural school system since kindergarten. Terrance lived with his single mother and his 23-year-old sister. The family lived below the poverty level, but Terrance's mother managed to provide a stable home life despite the difficulties that accompanied poverty. In fact, the entire community was economically depressed.

In high school, Terrance was placed in a self-contained special education classroom because of his weak academic skills and his tendency to speak loudly and to become angry when confronted with compliance by adult authority figures. In 9th grade a functional behavioral assessment was conducted and a behavioral intervention plan was implemented with some success. The summary follows:

Functional Behavioral Assessment/Behavioral Intervention Plan

Student: Terrance Young   Date: September 16   Grade: 9
Participants: Terrance Young, student; Ms. Young, parent; Mr. Logan, principal; Ms. Jones, special education supervisor; Ms. Hicks, special education teacher

A. PROBLEM IDENTIFICATION

1. Student strengths:
   Terrance is a very likable young man. He is outgoing and friendly. Terrance gets along well with peers and adults. Terrance has a 1-year-old daughter and another child due soon. He takes an active role in parenting.

2. List all of the student's behaviors of concern:
   Terrance has an inappropriate voice volume. He lacks self-control when faced with adversity. Terrance does not have self-motivation to complete high school.

3. Prioritize behaviors with selected target behavior:
   a. inappropriate voice volume
   b. lack of self control when faced with adversity
   c. lack of self-motivation

4. Previous interventions:

Intervention	Date Started	Date Ended	Reason Ended
School-based wraparound	Fall	Spring	Transition to high school
Social work	Fall	Ongoing	
Self-contained special classroom	Fall	Ongoing	
Token economy	Fall	Ongoing	
Level system	Fall	Ongoing	

5. Determine any long-term antecedents that may affect behavior:
   Parenting issues and family issues are present; there is tension between Terrance's girlfriend and her family. Terrance also has issues with male authority figures—he doesn't react well to punishment or correction.

6. Determine the antecedent and consequent events surrounding the behavior:

Antecedent	Behavior	Consequence
Faced with authority figure to redirect behavior	Verbal escalation	Gets in trouble with authority figure—loss of privileges

(continued)

Continued

7. Identify the function of the behavior:

Behavior	Communicative Function	Appropriate Replacement Behavior
Verbal escalation—verbally lashes out	Tries to assert himself—wants respect—wants to be heard	Remove himself from situation; express himself appropriately; could give him individual one-on-one time

8. Describe the desired behavior:
   Terrance will comply with adult requests in times of a redirection without any inappropriate verbal comments 90% of the time.

B. PLAN AND IMPLEMENTATION

1. Brainstorm possible solutions:
   a. Create positive environments that are less likely to include confrontation with authority figures where personalities conflict (e.g., enroll in classes with certain teachers).
   b. Pre correct the student about what to do when faced with authority figures.
   c. Implement a plan of escape to support student in avoiding verbal escalation.
   d. Practice how to respond in difficult situations.

2. Procedure for implementation:
   a. What happens if the desired behavior occurs?
      Behavior points reflect success; earn tokens for appropriate behaviors; phase out of more restrictive settings resulting in more freedom and more peer contact.
   b. What happens if the desired behavior does not occur?
      Teaching continues; student receives schoolwide discipline policy consequences; student loses points and may drop on behavior level system.
   c. What are criteria for success?
      Terrance will reach the highest level and choose to take special education classes within the cross-categorical program. Terrance will be successful at self-control when redirected.
   d. Maintenance:
      As Terrance transitions out of the self-contained special program, reinforcers are naturally faded.
   e. Home/school coordination plan:
      Use wraparound program.

3. Implementers:
   a. Classroom aide
   b. Special education teacher
   c. Social worker

4. Additional support needed:
   a. Classroom token economy works to provide incentives for behavior.
   b. Teacher monitors behavior.

Although Terrance appeared to transition successfully during the first half of 9th grade, he began to experience behavioral difficulties during second semester. At one point, he became involved in a verbal altercation with the physical education teacher. He was sent to the office and suspended for 5 school days. Despite the problem behaviors, Terrance made average grades in all classes and earned credit toward graduation. In 10th grade, however, a disciplinary incident occurred that would alter his education.

The disciplinary incident occurred on January 20 of Terrance's 10th grade year. On that day, Terrance was in the hallway walking to the cafeteria for lunch. Terrance had just lost lunchroom privileges because he used inappropriate and abusive language directed toward his special education teacher. Terrance was told to walk to the cafeteria, get his lunch, and return to the classroom to eat. Terrance walked down the hallway talking loudly about how he had been mistreated by the teacher. The principal, Mr. Logan, happened to overhear Terrance. As Mr. Logan confronted him, Terrance began to scream, yell, and verbally intimidate the principal. The classroom aide attempted to restrain Terrance, but was unsuccessful. The school police resource officer was called and removed Terrance. Terrance was searched and a small amount of marijuana was found in his pocket. Terrance was suspended from school for 10 days, with a possibility of expulsion.

An IEP meeting was held within the 10 days with Terrance's mother, the special education administrator, the principal, and the special education teacher. At the meeting, it was determined that Terrance would be placed in an interim alternative educational setting (IAES) for 45 school days. The IAES was determined to be home tutoring daily for 2 hours. Although Terrance's mother was unhappy about the placement, she did not protest. In addition, the following discussion occurred:

Ms. Jones: We have reviewed Terrance's IEP, discussed observations of Terrance at school, and reviewed all pertinent data about Terrance. Our consensus is that Terrance was receiving an appropriate education in the least restrictive environment. In fact, Terrance has been relatively successful since the behavioral intervention plan was put into effect. Does anyone have questions? (No one responded.) OK, we now need to address two questions to determine if Terrance's behavior was a manifestation of his disability. Was his conduct—that is, having drugs at school—caused by or did it have a direct and substantial relationship to his disability?

Ms. Hicks: I think I can provide input to answer this question. Terrance has a learning disability that affects his ability to read and he also lacks self-control when faced with pressure or an authority figure. These behaviors have been carefully documented and addressed in his IEP. I don't know what else we could do to help Terrance. He has never displayed any behavior that would indicate he was involved with drugs. I just don't understand why he brought drugs to school. He knows that this is illegal and against school policy. I don't think there is any relationship between his disability and the behavior of bringing drugs to school.

Ms. Young: I am so unhappy with Terrance's behavior! You all were doing what you could to help him and now he does this! I can't feel sorry for him and I just don't know what to do with him!

(Other participants agreed with Ms. Hicks and Ms. Young.)

Ms. Jones: It appears that we are in agreement that Terrance's behavior of bringing drugs to school was not related to his disability. Now, was his behavior the direct result of the school's failure to implement his IEP?

Ms. Hicks: Absolutely not! All services that Terrance needed were carefully documented in his IEP and he received every service.

Mr. Logan: I completely agree. Everyone who worked with Terrance was aware of what he needed and he received all services in his IEP.

Ms. Jones: Then we are in agreement that the school implemented his IEP. Therefore, Terrance's behavior is not a manifestation of his disability. As we previously discussed, Terrance will be placed in an interim alternative educational setting for 45 days and will receive the services outlined in his IEP. During the next few weeks, the school district will hold an expulsion hearing. If he is expelled, he will not return to the high school. If he is not expelled, he will return to his current placement on the 46th day after beginning the interim alternative educational setting. The discussion held today will be presented at the expulsion hearing.

The meeting concluded and Terrance began receiving special education services daily for 2 hours at his home. An expulsion hearing was held and it was recommended to the board of education that Terrance be expelled for bringing drugs to school. The board of education decided to expel Terrance for the next school year. In addition, an IEP meeting was held to determine what services Terrance would require to continue to work toward his IEP goals. Ultimately, Terrance was placed in a private day treatment facility where his learning disability and behavior problems could be addressed.

Legal Issues

1. What did school district personnel consider, to determine whether Terrance's behavior was a manifestation of his disability? Did the LEA legally follow the correct procedure? How do you know?

2. Was the LEA correct in placing Terrance in an IAES and then expelling Terrance? How do you know?

3. Did the LEA legally have to continue providing Terrance an education? How does the law address this issue?

Other Issues

1. If Terrance had engaged in similar behavior outside of the school setting with a shop owner, what would have happened? What are the differences between this scenario and the same scenario in the school setting?

2. Is it possible that Terrance could have a learning disability? Why or why not?

Activity

Interview a school police resource officer and ask him or her the questions posed under "Other Issues." Discuss in a small group the differences in opinion.

Chapter **6**

Nondiscriminatory Assessment

CASE 6.1   Carlos

Major issue: Accommodations

Secondary issue: State assessment

Characters

Mark Kuchta, special education teacher

Carlos Otero, 11th-grade student with learning disability

Mark Kuchta:

I pulled the note from my school mailbox in February. It read:

Dear Mark:

As you know, we are required to administer the state test in March to all students in 11th grade. This includes your students (in special education). Because you are the English teacher in special education, it is your responsibility to administer the test to your students. I will distribute test materials 2 days before the test, but you will receive instructions on administration in the next few weeks. Our guidance counselors will develop the schedule for testing during the week of March 12. You should provide accommodations for your students in special education. If you have questions, don't hesitate to see me.

James McPherson, Principal

As a new special education teacher in this high school, I wasn't quite sure what to do. Because this was a small high school, I was the only special education teacher who taught English to students with disabilities. Most of my students were in my class because they were poor readers and had poor writing skills. However, I really was concerned about Carlos taking the test.

Carlos was labeled "emotionally disturbed," but I did not have any problems with his behavior. Carlos was a nonreader. This was his real disability. I have never seen a child at this age who was a nonreader. Carlos carried an ID in his wallet that contained his address and telephone number. When asked to write his name and address, he had to copy, letter for letter, from the ID card. Carlos could not recognize any words in print, either by sight or by phonetic analysis. He seemed quite bright and understood many concepts, but he couldn't even order food in a fast food restaurant because of his reading disability. In English class, I allowed Carlos to listen as other students read aloud our reading selections. I usually read tests aloud to Carlos and made accommodations as needed.

As I thought about how I would administer the state test, I worried about Carlos. It would be impossible to administer the test to Carlos in my English class because he wouldn't be able to follow along as quickly as the other students. I had already decided that I would read the test to the class, but Carlos would need more assistance. I reviewed his IEP and determined that there wasn't much guidance to assist me in deciding how to help Carlos. The section of the IEP that dealt with assessment read as follows:

Participation in State and Local Assessments

Grade placement of student: 11th grade

The student will:

___ Participate in the entire state assessment with no accommodations
_X_ Participate in the entire state assessment with accommodations
___ Participate in part(s) of the state assessment (specified below)
___ Not participate in the state assessment

___ Participate in the entire districtwide assessment with no accommodations
_X_ Participate in the entire districtwide assessment with accommodations
___ Participate in part(s) of the districtwide assessment (specified below)
___ Not participate in the districtwide assessment

If the student is completing the assessment(s) with accommodations, specify the needed accommodations.

Carlos will be provided accommodations as necessary.

After reviewing the IEP, I made several decisions on what accommodations would be used with Carlos. Because Carlos was somewhat distractible, I would change his English class to the hour when I had my planning period during testing. Then I could administer the test individually and schedule frequent breaks. I also decided to administer the test in a small office in the building. Because Carlos had a significant reading disability, I would read the test to him. Although he had strong skills in math, I would allow him to use a calculator so that he wouldn't become frustrated. Because he had difficulty writing, I would let him write in the test booklet instead of the response sheet. Finally, for the writing test, I would allow him to verbalize his essays and transcribe for him in writing. These accommodations had been successful with other students who had significant learning disabilities, so I knew they would be appropriate for Carlos. I would use all of the accommodations for all of the subtests, which included reading, mathematics, and written language.

I made the necessary arrangements and talked with Carlos, who agreed to allow me to administer the test individually with necessary accommodations. During the week of testing, Carlos seemed relieved to work with me by himself. He was very cooperative and I even coached him a little when he seemed to know the answer, but couldn't quite choose correctly. For all other students with disabilities, I administered the test in their special education English class. I used similar accommodations with these students—like reading the test aloud, allowing frequent breaks, permitting use of a calculator, and writing in the test booklet instead of the response sheet. The only accommodation that did not work was transcribing oral responses for the writing test. With just one teacher in the classroom, this just wouldn't work.

Several months later, the school received the results for the state test. Our school did not meet adequate yearly progress because of the performance of our students in special education. During the previous year, 19% of students in special education met the standards in reading, 23% in mathematics, and 15% in writing. This year, 15% of students in special education met the standards in reading, 24% in mathematics, and 13% in writing.

Legal Issues

1. To what extent were the assessment accommodations used with Carlos properly determined?
2. To what extent were the assessment accommodations used with Carlos legally documented?

Other Issues

1. Should every student with a learning disability receive the same assessment accommodations? Why or why not?

2. To what extent should assessment accommodations and instructional accommodations be connected?

3. Discuss the appropriateness of assessment accommodations that were used with Carlos.

Activity

Review the Web site for your state's assessment system. What guidance is given in providing accommodations for students with disabilities?

CASE 6.2   Anna

Major issue: Eligibility

Secondary issue: Response to intervention

Characters

Anna Kowalski, 8-year-old child with possible learning disability

Mrs. Kowalski, Anna's mother

Mr. Kiena, school psychologist

Ms. Liu, 3rd-grade teacher

Mr. Scott, special education teacher

Mr. Stevens, school social worker

Ms. Miller, principal

Ms. Denman, special education administrator

Note: This case has been written to present two different scenarios regarding Anna's evaluation for special education services.

Scenario 1

The participants at the IEP team meeting gathered around the principal's conference table on Friday at 8 a.m. After introductions were quickly made, Ms. Denman, the special education administrator, began the meeting: "As we know, Anna was referred for a special education evaluation on January 15. We are here today to review the results of the evaluation that was completed, determine if Anna is eligible for special education services, and appropriately plan for Anna in school. Ms. Liu, you have been Anna's teacher this year and you initiated the referral for special education. Would you please tell us how Anna has progressed in your class this year?"

Ms. Liu answered, "There is only so much I can do with Anna in the classroom. She constantly struggles with reading. In 3rd grade, students are expected to complete independent tasks using reading, but Anna just can't complete the assignments because of her poor reading ability. She turns in assignments partially completed and doesn't write in cursive. When I ask her if she needs help, she says she doesn't need anything. In reading class, we are beginning to read a novel. Students take turns reading aloud. I try to avoid putting Anna on the spot to read aloud because she stumbles over most of the words. I just can't give her individual attention in reading with 25 other students in the class. I think Anna needs help!"

Ms. Denman said, "Thank you, Ms. Liu. Mr. Stevens, you met with Mrs. Kowalski recently. Would you summarize your report?"

Mr. Stevens began, "Yes. Mrs. Kowalski and I met last week to discuss Anna's health and social history. Anna lives with her mother, Mrs. Kowalski, in an apartment. There are no other relatives in the area and Mrs. Kowalski and Anna have lived alone since Anna's father left the family when Anna was 3 years old. Anna has not experienced any physical problems out of the ordinary. She passed a recent hearing and vision test. At home, Mrs. Kowalski reports that Anna has become responsible for a number of household chores like setting the table, washing dishes, cleaning her room, and sometimes cooking. Mrs. Kowalski recently took a new job and works long hours, often not getting home until after 6 p.m. She reports that her new job is exhausting and that Anna must help around the house. Homework is completed, but often Anna works by herself. Mrs. Kowalski reported that she is very concerned about Anna's progress in school, but that she doesn't know how to help. Mrs. Kowalski, would you like to add anything else?"

Mrs. Kowalski shook her head.

Ms. Denman moved to Mr. Kiena, the school psychologist, asking, "Mr. Kiena, you evaluated Anna. Would you summarize your test results?"

Mr. Kiena began the report by summarizing Anna's reported progress in school as summarized by her teachers, present and previous, and her grades. She was currently failing her reading and language arts classes and earning below average grades in other classes. Mr. Kiena then summarized his test results by saying, "I saw Anna 2 weeks ago and administered a standardized intelligence test, the Wechsler Intelligence Scale for Children, Fourth Edition. On this test, Anna's overall ability was within the low average range. On the four indexes assessed—verbal comprehension, perceptual reasoning, working memory, and processing speed—Anna performed within the low average range. There was no significant difference between any of the scores. When I administered the Wechsler Individual Achievement Test, Second Edition, Anna was assessed in reading, mathematics, spelling, written expression, listening comprehension, and oral expression. On all of these tests, Anna functioned within the low average range, which is about $1\frac{1}{2}$ to 2 years below grade level. She is performing exactly as well as we would expect, given her overall ability. There is no significant discrepancy between her ability and her level of academic achievement. Therefore, I do not think she has a learning disability. She learns at a slower rate than other children."

Ms. Liu was unhappy with the outcome of the assessment. However, Ms. Denman clearly stated that a child could not be identified with learning disabilities if a significant discrepancy between achievement and potential was not evident. Mrs. Kowalski did not say anything. The team concluded by stating that Anna was not eligible for special education services and that the teacher would have to continue working with her as best she could in reading.

Scenario 2

After the IEP team gathered around the conference table in the principal's office, introductions were made, but it was evident that the team knew each other. Ms. Denman began the meeting by reviewing Anna's case: "As you know, we have been working with Anna since the end of 1st grade through our building-based support team. When we first began working with her, Anna was given a series of assessments to determine her functional level in reading. The team then provided targeted interventions in reading, tracking her progress. The team met several times to review Anna's progress and to change or alter interventions. In late November, it became apparent to the team that Anna was not making adequate progress despite the interventions. Mrs. Kowalski, you have been working with the team since last year, and in November you agreed that Anna needed further evaluation to determine if she needed more intensive, individualized interventions. This is why we are here today. We will review Anna's progress, additional evaluations, and determine if Anna needs more services. Mr. Kiena, would you discuss the assessments and evaluations?"

Mr. Kiena began by talking about the initial assessments in reading from last year: "Anna was initially administered a series of assessments, called Dynamic Indicators of Basic Early Literacy Skills—DIBELS—toward the end of 1st grade. The team working with her was concerned about her reading achievement and skill development. Anna clearly had difficulty with oral reading fluency, nonsense word fluency, and phonemic segmentation fluency. As a team, we determined several intensive reading interventions, using phonemic awareness and phonics as the target skills needed. We recommended a 6-week summer school program in reading and then continued interventions during 2nd grade. While there was some improvement noted in phonemic awareness and basic phonics skills, Anna still struggles in her reading class. Anna continues, despite the best efforts from the team, to experience considerable difficulty in reading fluency. Our team, including Mrs. Kowalski, worked very well together on behalf of Anna."

Ms. Liu continued, "Mrs. Kowalski and I continued working as members of the team to help Anna in reading this year. I completely agree that Anna may be in need of more intensive assistance. She really works well within the classroom, but I think more intensive assistance in reading might make a difference. Mrs. Kowalski, do you have anything to add?"

Mrs. Kowalski began, "I really appreciate the support that the teachers have given to Anna. As you know, I work long hours at a new job and I don't often get home until at least 6 p.m. Anna has learned to become more independent. I do try every evening to work with her in reading, even if it is just for 10 minutes. However, in 3rd grade, I can see that it is more difficult for her to keep up with the class. I agree that she needs more help."

Other team members reported updated information about Anna's progress, including psychological assessments that showed Anna's overall ability to be within the low average range and achievement assessments that were consistent with her abilities. Mr. Stevens, also a member of the support team, reviewed an update of the family and health history, including a recent vision and hearing screening, which Anna passed.

The team consensus was to provide Anna with a higher intensity level of services, based on her individual needs in reading. This meant that Anna was eligible for special education services under the label "learning disability." The team wrote an individualized education program for Anna that included continuation of previous in-classroom interventions and they added the services of the special education teacher, Mr. Scott, for individualized reading instruction. Mr. Scott would work with Anna daily within the classroom to support her reading and also see Anna outside of the classroom in a very small group for intensive, specialized reading instruction. The team agreed to track Anna's progress weekly and communicate with Mrs. Kowalski frequently. The team would meet formally to review Anna's progress in May. Mrs. Kowalski signed an informed consent for Anna to receive the services and expressed her appreciation to the team.

Legal Issues

1. Describe the basis used for making the eligibility decision in scenario 1, then scenario 2. To what extent was each eligibility decision legal according to IDEA?

2. Describe the assessments used in each scenario. To what extent was each evaluation full, individualized, and comprehensive?

Other Issues

1. Why wasn't Anna eligible for learning disability services in the first scenario? Why was Anna eligible for learning disability services in the second scenario?

2. Discuss the definition of *severe discrepancy* and *response to intervention* and tell how each contributed to making the eligibility decision in each scenario.

Activity

Using the chart below, describe each factor and discuss its contribution to the outcome of each meeting. Compare and contrast the two scenarios. Which would you prefer and why?

	Scenario 1	Scenario 2
Prereferral (i.e., building-based support team)		
Referral		
Assessments used		
Criteria for learning disabilities/eligibility decision		
Parent participation		

Chapter 7

Appropriate Education and Individualized Education Programs

CASE 7.1 Thomas

Major issue: Transition

Secondary issue: Free appropriate public education (FAPE)

Characters

Ali Young, high school special education teacher

Thomas Ross, high school student with disabilities

Ali Young:

My annual reviews were scheduled for next week. I was responsible for writing the individualized education programs (IEPs) for 20 students at our high school and I was released from my teaching schedule for one day to prepare. I was almost finished, but I just wasn't sure how I would approach Thomas's IEP.

As I reviewed his file, I noted that Thomas had multiple moderate to severe disabilities. His primary disability was visual impairment, as he had a congenital condition that caused retinal degeneration in both eyes. He was legally blind and his vision was deteriorating. In addition, Thomas had a significant cognitive delay, central auditory processing disorder, speech and language delay, and occasionally had seizures.

I worked with Thomas one hour a day to support his placement in regular education classes. In addition to support from me in special education, Thomas had a full-time educational assistant and received services from the teacher of the visually impaired and the speech and language therapist. Thomas worked so hard and everyone who worked with him said he was a joy to have in class. Thomas always displayed appropriate behavior and he seemed to have positive relationships with his peer group. Thomas earned A's and B's in most classes and his grades were mostly based on effort.

My real concern was that Thomas wasn't receiving appropriate services to help him become independent after he graduated from high school. His curriculum was completely tied to the general education academic curriculum and his parents were very supportive of this placement. I wondered how struggling through reading a novel written on a high school reading level would enable him to hold a job or to live independently. It seemed that Thomas was placed in the regular education classroom just because his parents wanted him to socialize with other students. The academic work had to be modified beyond recognition. For example, Thomas did not have the skill level to read *To Kill a Mockingbird* in his English class, so the book was read aloud to him and he was allowed to write partial answers to comprehension questions in Braille with support from the assistant.

As I reviewed Thomas's previous IEP, I wondered how it could be changed to better meet his needs. In part, his previous IEP included the following components:

Individualized Education Program

Name: Thomas Ross   Grade: 9   Parent(s): Ms. Nancy Ross
Address: 105 Blueridge Drive   Date of IEP: May 15

PARTICIPANTS:

Ms. Young, Special Education Teacher
(Ms. Ross was invited, but did not attend)

CURRENT LEVELS OF PERFORMANCE:

1. Academic: Thomas functions on a 2nd-grade level in reading (can read simple stories in Braille). He can write a 5-sentence paragraph with many spelling and mechanics errors using his Braille machine. He can add and subtract 2-digit numbers.

2. Social/emotional: Thomas has a high tolerance for frustration. He works well with other students and is well liked by both peers and adults. He is enthusiastic and motivated.

3. Independent functioning: Thomas needs the support of an adult at all times to help with academic tasks and to maneuver around the school building.

4. Speech/language/communication: Thomas has a central auditory processing disorder, resulting in difficulty processing language. His speech is difficult to understand.

5. Vocational skills: Thomas is not engaged in vocational activity.

6. Motor skills: Thomas can use the Braille machine to write. Gross motor skills are age-appropriate.

7. Other: Thomas has a degenerative condition causing retinal degeneration in both eyes. He is legally blind and uses Braille. He has a significant cognitive delay. Thomas has occasional seizures and takes medication to control them.

ANNUAL GOALS:

Goal type: __X__ Annual __X__ Transition
Goal statement: Thomas will read a novel appropriate for high school students and answer comprehension questions using a Braille machine and assistance from the aide.
Implementer: Special education teacher/regular education teacher
Projected completion date: May

Monitoring Schedule	Evaluation Procedures	Criteria for Mastery
Daily _____	Tests __X__	71%–81% accuracy __X__
Weekly _____	Charting _____	81%–90% accuracy _____
Monthly _____	Observations _____	91%–100% accuracy _____
Quarterly _____	Daily log _____	_____ of _____ trials _____
Grade period __X__	Other _____	Other _____
Other _____		

Goal Type: __X__ Annual __X__ Transition
Goal statement: Thomas will complete addition and subtraction problems using 3 and 4 digits with borrowing and carrying.
Implementer: Special education teacher/regular education teacher
Projected completion date: May

Monitoring Schedule	Evaluation Procedures	Criteria for Mastery
Daily _____	Tests __X__	71%–81% accuracy __X__
Weekly _____	Charting _____	81%–90% accuracy _____
Monthly _____	Observations _____	91%–100% accuracy _____
Quarterly _____	Daily log _____	_____ of _____ trials _____
Grade period __X__	Other _____	Other _____
Other _____		

General education modifications/adaptations/supplemental aids and services and/or supports for school personnel:

Subject Area (academic and nonacademic)	Explanation of General Education Modifications/Adaptations/ Supplemental Aids and Services and/or Supports for School Personnel	Special Education Support Necessary? (If yes, specify.)
Cafeteria	Needs aide to assist with mobility	Yes: full-time aide
Movement through hallways, to/from bus, restroom	Needs aide to assist with mobility	Yes: full-time aide
English	Read tests aloud; allow Braille responses in writing; Braille textbooks; modify worksheets to simplify and write in	Yes: full-time aide

(continued)

(Continued)

	Braille; needs aide to assist in completing academic tasks, extended time, fewer assignments	
Algebra	Read tests aloud; allow Braille responses in writing; Braille textbooks; modify worksheets to simplify and write in Braille; needs aide to assist in completing academic tasks, extended time, fewer assignments	Yes: full-time aide
Civics	Read tests aloud; allow Braille responses in writing; Braille textbooks; modify worksheets to simplify and write in Braille; needs aide to assist in completing academic tasks, extended time, fewer assignments	Yes: full-time aide
Biology	Read tests aloud; allow Braille responses in writing; Braille textbooks; modify worksheets to simplify and write in Braille; needs aide to assist in completing academic tasks, extended time, fewer assignments	Yes: full-time aide

Special education and related services:

Needed Service	Location of Service	Minutes per Day	Date of Initiation of Service	Anticipated Duration	Frequency of Service
Learning disabilities tutoring	Special education classroom	60	Sept. 1	May 30	Daily
Individual aide	Regular education classroom; mobility throughout building	360	Sept. 1	May 30	Daily
Services of teacher of visually impaired	Special education classroom	60	Sept. 1	May 30	Twice a week
Speech/ language services	Special education classroom	20	Sept. 1	May 30	Twice a week

Extent to which student will not participate with nondisabled children in the regular class and in nonacademic/extracurricular activities:

Thomas will eat lunch in the cafeteria and walk through the halls with assistance from the aide. He will participate in all general academic subjects. Parents want him fully integrated with nondisabled peers.

TRANSITION PLAN:

Postschool vision (including employment, education, and living arrangements):
Thomas does not know what he wants to do when he leaves school. The parents want him fully integrated with nondisabled peers.

Course of study:
Year 1: Regular education academic program with support
Year 2: _____
Year 3: _____
Year 4: _____
Other: _____

Annual needed services:
Instruction: __X__ Yes _____ No
Regular education academic courses with special education support

Community experiences: _____ Yes __X__ No
Not needed at this time

Employment and other postschool adult living objectives: _____ Yes __X__ No
Not needed at this time

As appropriate, daily living skills and functional vocational evaluation: _____ Yes __X__ No
Not needed at this time

If appropriate, a statement of each outside agency's responsibility, or linkage before the student leaves the school setting:
Not applicable

PARTICIPATION IN STATE AND LOCAL ASSESSMENTS:

Grade placement of student: 9
The student will:
_____ Participate in the entire state assessment with no accommodations.
__X__ Participate in the entire state assessment with accommodations.
_____ Participate in part(s) of the state assessment (as specified below).
_____ Not participate in the state assessment.*
_____ Participate in the entire districtwide assessment with no accommodations.
__X__ Participate in the entire districtwide assessment with accommodations.
_____ Participate in part(s) of the districtwide assessment (as specified below).
_____ Not participate in the districtwide assessment.*

(continued)

(Continued)

If the student is completing the assessment(s) with accommodations, specify the needed accommodations:

Braille test
Use Braille machine for written responses that require short answer or essay
Read test aloud (except reading)
Extended time
Alternate setting (special education classroom)

*Rationale for decision: _____

_____

_____

After reviewing Thomas's recent IEP, I compared it with previous IEPs. I noted that the goals had not changed since 4th grade. I really think that we are not programming appropriately for Thomas. Instead of listening to his aide read *To Kill a Mockingbird*, he should be learning functional daily living skills. I don't think Thomas is really earning A's and B's based on his knowledge. Isn't this dishonest to give him above average grades? Shouldn't he really be placed in a special education program where his needs can truly be met?

Legal Issues

1. Did the school district comply with correct procedures in writing the IEP discussed in this case? What evidence supports your position?
2. Was Thomas's IEP reasonably calculated to provide educational benefits? How do you know? You may want to review goals, services, and the transition plan.
3. Was Thomas's IEP individually written to meet his needs? How do you know?

Other Issues

1. What potential effect did Thomas's performance on the state test have on whether or not the school met adequate yearly progress?
2. At what point should a student's purely academic curriculum (tied to the general education curriculum) be changed to a functional curriculum?
3. Do you agree with the position of the special education teacher? Why or why not?

Activity

You are the special education teacher attending Thomas's next IEP meeting. Prior to the meeting, you are writing a draft of the proposed IEP for next year. Using the form below, complete an appropriate and legal draft IEP for Thomas:

Individualized Education Program

Name: Thomas Ross   Grade: 10   Parent(s): Ms. Nancy Ross
Address: 105 Blueridge Drive   Date of IEP: May 15

PARTICIPANTS:

_____   _____   _____

_____   _____   _____

CURRENT LEVELS OF PERFORMANCE (see IEP in case).
ANNUAL GOALS:

Goal type: _____ Annual _____ Transition

Goal statement: _____

_____

_____

Implementer: _____

Projected completion date: _____

Monitoring Schedule	Evaluation Procedures	Criteria for Mastery
Daily _____	Tests _____	71%–81% accuracy _____
Weekly _____	Charting _____	81%–90% accuracy _____
Monthly _____	Observations _____	91%–100% accuracy _____
Quarterly _____	Daily log _____	_____ of _____ trials _____
Grade period _____	Other _____	Other _____
Other _____		

Goal Type: _____ Annual _____ Transition

Goal Statement: _____

_____

_____

Implementer: _____

Projected completion date: _____

(continued)

Monitoring Schedule	Evaluation Procedures	Criteria for Mastery
Daily ____	Tests ____	71%–81% accuracy ____
Weekly ____	Charting ____	81%–90% accuracy ____
Monthly ____	Observations ____	91%–100% accuracy ____
Quarterly ____	Daily log ____	____ of ____ trials ____
Grade period ____	Other ____	Other ____
Other ____		

General education modifications/adaptations/supplemental aids and services and/or supports for school personnel:

Subject Area (academic and nonacademic)	Explanation of General Education Modifications/ Adaptations/Supplemental Aids and Services and/or Supports for School Personnel	Special Education Support Necessary? (If yes, specify.)

Special education and related services:

Needed Service	Location of Service	Minutes per Day	Date of Initiation of Service	Anticipated Duration	Frequency of Service

Extent to which student will not participate with nondisabled children in the regular class and in nonacademic/extracurricular activities: _____
_____
_____

TRANSITION PLAN:

Postschool vision (including employment, education, and living arrangements): _____
_____
_____

Course of study:

Year 1: _____

Year 2: _____

Year 3: _____

Year 4: _____

Other: _____

(*Continued*)
Annual needed services:
Instruction: ___Yes ___No

Community Experiences: ___Yes ___No

Employment and other postschool adult living objectives: ___Yes ___No

As appropriate, daily living skills and functional vocational evaluation: ___Yes ___No

If appropriate, a statement of each outside agency's responsibility, or linkage before the student leaves the school setting: _____
_____
_____

PARTICIPATION IN STATE AND LOCAL ASSESSMENTS:

Grade placement of student: 10
The student will:
___Participate in the entire state assessment with no accommodations.
___Participate in the entire state assessment with accommodations.
___Participate in part(s) of the state assessment (as specified below).
___Not participate in the state assessment.*
___Participate in the entire districtwide assessment with no accommodations.
___Participate in the entire districtwide assessment with accommodations.
___Participate in part(s) of the districtwide assessment (as specified below).
___Not participate in the districtwide assessment.*

If the student is completing the assessment(s) with accommodations, specify the needed accommodations: _____
_____

* Rationale for decision: _____
_____
_____

CASE 7.2   Jacob

Major issue: Free appropriate public education (FAPE)
Secondary issue: Individualized education program (IEP)

Characters

Mary Li, hearing officer

Jacob Pulse, 3-year-old child with autism

Julie and Bill Pulse, parents

Marsha Brown, special education administrator

Mary Li had been a state hearing officer for the past 3 years, and each year the issues seemed to become more emotional and complicated. Her recent case was the most difficult. After hearing almost 5 days of testimony from both parent and school district witnesses, she now had to review the facts and files concerning Jacob's history, his evaluation, and the proposed IEP—and then issue a decision.

History

Jacob was a 3-year-old boy with mild to moderate autism or pervasive developmental delay. He was formally diagnosed at around age 2, but he displayed autistic characteristics when he developed a serious viral infection that resulted in hospitalization at 8 months of age. Right after the hospitalization, Jacob completely stopped talking. Up to that point, he spoke some words and babbled. Jacob's parents began an applied behavioral analysis (ABA) program at home when Jacob was 2 years old as recommended by a private psychologist. The program was an intensive one that focused on increasing attention memory. It consisted of 42 hours of one-to-one therapy each week (6 hours a day, 7 days a week). Jacob's parents also arranged for occupational therapy twice a week and speech-language therapy three times a week. Jacob's parents paid for the ABA therapy and their health insurance paid for the related therapies. Both parents and their private psychologist were very pleased with the huge gains in the home-based ABA program and related therapies. It was focused and successful with Jacob.

Evaluation

Prior to Jacob's 3rd birthday, Mrs. Pulse met with the special education administrator, Ms. Brown. They discussed conducting an evaluation, and consent was obtained. Arrangements were also made for Mrs. Pulse to observe in the half-day early childhood classroom and a full-day private school program for children with autism. Over the next 6 weeks, an evaluation was completed. The evaluation included, in part, the following components:

- Play-based assessment, because Jacob had difficulty sitting for formal testing (Play activities were presented to Jacob with the parents, psychologist, occupational therapist, and speech-language therapist observing. The assessment measured Jacob's communication skills, social interaction, cognitive verbal and nonverbal skills, and motor skills.)
- Review of records provided from the parents, including information about Jacob's current in-home ABA program and related therapies
- Medical, social, and family history

IEP Meeting

After completion of the evaluation, the IEP team met to discuss the results. The speech-language therapist indicated that Jacob said a few words, but had minimal verbal expression skills. The occupational therapist stated that Jacob had low muscle tone, making it difficult to maintain posture against gravity, and that he had difficulty with fine motor skills such as using scissors. The school psychologist indicated that Jacob was developmentally delayed in cognitive skill development, pragmatic social skills, fine motor skills, and communication skills. Jacob was also easily distracted and had difficulty following directions. The IEP team agreed that Jacob had the disability of autism, and that he required special education and related services. At this point, the team drafted goals for Jacob that addressed fine motor skills, sensory input, attentiveness, social interactions, following directions, maintaining eye contact, and communication skills.

Proposed IEP

One option was considered by the IEP team: placement in the early childhood classroom for $2\frac{1}{2}$ hours per day ($12\frac{1}{2}$ hours per week). The team recommended this placement with related services, including 90 minutes per week of speech-language therapy, 60 minutes per week of occupational therapy, and 30 minutes per week of social work. The team decided that this option was appropriate given the difficulty of Jacob's transition to a school setting.

When questioned about the methodology used in the early childhood classroom, the teacher discussed a variety of educational methods, depending upon individual needs—including discrete trial training and PECS (picture exchange communication system). The discrete trial method focused on teaching a task through repetition (task is taught, an instruction is given to the child, a prompt is provided, and response is elicited from the child). PECS was incorporated as a communication strategy, giving the child a method to communicate using pictures. Both methods were individualized and could be applied to any child regardless of where the child functioned on the autism spectrum. The methods were widely accepted and research based.

Both parents accepted the related services, but declined the special education early childhood classroom services. They requested continuation of the in-home ABA program. The district personnel argued that the proposed program was individualized and tailored for children who were autistic. The parents stated that $12\frac{1}{2}$ hours of instruction per week was not intense enough, and that $27\frac{1}{2}$ hours per week was the minimum acceptable.

The school district personnel and parents did not dispute the procedures used to evaluate Jacob, the procedures used to schedule the IEP meeting, or the sufficiency of the proposed goals. But they did not agree on the proposed placement. The meeting concluded without parental agreement or consent. The parents requested a due process hearing and asked that the school district provide funding for the in-home ABA program.

Now Mary Li had to issue a decision order to the school district and the parents.

Legal Issues

1. To what extent did the school district offer a free appropriate public education in the least restrictive environment? Was the IEP reasonably calculated to confer educational benefit?

2. To what extent does the school district have to defer to the parent in terms of educational methodology? Should the school district have incorporated ABA into the school setting? Why or why not?

Other Issues

1. What, if anything, do you think the school district should have done to gain consensus at the IEP meeting?

2. At what point should a school district firmly stand behind the IEP team decision?

Activity

You are the hearing officer in this case. Write a decision order to the school district and parents. Make sure that you include the specific decision and legal rationale used by addressing these issues:

* Individualized IEP
* Least restrictive environment

- Free appropriate public education
- Methodology

Begin your order with the following statement: *There is no question that Jacob benefited from the at-home ABA program and that ABA is a well-researched methodology. ABA may even be a superior methodology, but the question is: Can Jacob gain educational benefit from the proposed program? The school district is ordered to . . .*

Chapter **8**

Least Restrictive Environment

CASE 8.1 Rhonda

Major issue: Individualized education program (IEP)
Secondary issue: Accommodations

Characters

> Rhonda Smith, 3rd-grade student with learning disability
> Tranita Jackson, 3rd-grade regular education teacher
> Lakisha Mills, special education teacher

Rhonda's IEP meeting was very difficult. Rhonda was in 3rd grade and failing almost all classes. In October, she was referred for a special education evaluation and was determined to have a learning disability. The IEP team deliberated for a lengthy time determining exactly what services Rhonda needed and, although consensus was reached, Tranita Jackson, the 3rd-grade teacher, was not convinced that the IEP was in Rhonda's best interest. She really felt that Rhonda should have been placed in the self-contained special education class for all academic subjects. Rhonda struggled with reading and functioned at a beginning 2nd-grade level. Rhonda was just learning cursive letters, but the rest of the class used cursive writing fluently. Rhonda had difficulty writing a paragraph, but the rest of the class was writing three-paragraph essays. However, Rhonda demonstrated above average verbal skills and mathematics skills, especially in the area of verbal problem solving. In class discussions, she excelled verbally. The majority of the IEP team felt that Rhonda would benefit from remaining in the regular education classroom and that she needed special accommodations and adaptations, along with support from the special education teacher. The accommodations/adaptations/supports included the following:

* Extra time allotted for tests and quizzes
* Tests and quizzes for social studies and science read aloud in the special education classroom
* Study guides created by the special education teacher, with the regular education teacher providing content in social studies and science to the special education teacher one week in advance
* Use of a computer for written assignments
* An extra set of textbooks for the parents to use at home
* Requirement that Rhonda be "checked out" at the end of each day by the special education teacher to make sure all assignments are written in her planner
* Preferential seating within the regular classroom in the front of the room

Rhonda also was to receive intensive reading instruction in a very small group setting on a daily basis in the special education classroom to supplement the instruction in the regular education classroom. This reading instruction was to focus on phonemic awareness and phonics skills.

The first problem occurred when Lakisha Mills, the special education teacher, asked the 3rd-grade teacher, Ms. Jackson, for the study materials in social studies and science for the upcoming week so that she could create a study guide. Ms. Jackson said, "We will cover chapter 6 in science and chapter 5 in social studies. You have a copy of the textbooks." Ms. Mills requested more detail about the content, but her request was ignored.

Ms. Mills then created an outline and study guide for the upcoming chapters in the textbooks. However, the next week in the 3rd-grade classroom, Ms. Jackson conducted a science experiment that was not discussed in the textbook and began a completely different unit in social studies. Rhonda did not understand the vocabulary or procedures in the science experiment, and the special education teacher was at a loss to help her after the experiment had been conducted. When approached about the science activity and different unit in the 3rd-grade social studies class, Ms. Jackson answered that she thought she had told Ms. Mills about the change. When given a quiz over the material at the end of the week on the science experiment and social studies content, Rhonda took both within the regular education classroom and received an F on each.

Ms. Mills was very upset, but continued to work with Rhonda. However, it became very difficult following an incident that involved Rhonda's check-out time in the special education class during the last period of the day. The intent was to make sure Rhonda had all assignments written in her planner. But every day, Rhonda either didn't attend or was at least 30 minutes late, leaving only a few minutes for the task at hand. After several days, Ms. Mills walked to the 3rd-grade classroom to find out why Rhonda was late. As Ms. Mills entered the classroom, Ms. Jackson was teaching a lesson in spelling. Ms. Mills stood quietly at the door and waited for a pause in the instruction, then said to Ms. Jackson, "May I talk to you?"

Ms. Jackson turned her back to the special education teacher and said loudly to the class, "I can tell that we are going to be interrupted again today. This time, we are interrupted by Ms. Mills and I know what she wants. Rhonda, please gather your binder and go with Ms. Mills. I just keep forgetting to send you to her room. Rhonda, you can make up this spelling work in Ms. Mills's classroom. Remember, your spelling sentences are due tomorrow." Ms. Mills felt embarrassed and humiliated, but left the classroom with Rhonda.

Later that day after school, Ms. Mills went into the 3rd-grade classroom. She said, "Tranita, we need to talk about Rhonda's IEP. I feel that I am not getting any cooperation in providing the services outlined on Rhonda's IEP. Every day, Rhonda is late for the last period for check-out and I have not yet received the correct material in advance to develop study guides for science and social studies. Rhonda has been receiving several F's in her work as a direct result of not receiving assistance."

Ms. Jackson looked surprised as she said, "I always try to help all of my students. I told you in the IEP meeting that Rhonda could not be successful in my class and her grades demonstrate that she cannot complete the work. Her time is too fragmented. With her schedule, I cannot even change my lessons to meet the needs of my class. I feel like you are following me around all of the time. It is more work to provide you with information to help Rhonda than it is to help her myself. I really don't want anyone else in my classroom, Lakisha. Either move Rhonda out of my classroom to the special education classroom, or let me teach Rhonda just like I teach all of my other students."

Ms. Mills was very upset as she quickly walked out of Ms. Jackson's classroom. As she left, she said she would request an IEP meeting.

After 2 weeks, another IEP meeting was held. Ms. Jackson stated that Rhonda was not successful in the 3rd-grade classroom and that she needed all of her academic instruction in the special education classroom. Rhonda's mother agreed and requested that the change be reflected in the IEP. Ms. Mills tried to state her objection and said that the services Rhonda needed could be delivered within the regular classroom—but no one listened or agreed. Even the building principal agreed to the self-contained special education classroom. The IEP was changed so that Rhonda would receive all academic instruction in Ms. Mills's special education classroom, but attend art, music, and physical education with the regular education 3rd-grade class. In addition, the team determined that Rhonda would take the state test with accommodations within the special education classroom. Accommodations included alternate test site, reading the test to Rhonda (except the reading test), and extended time. Coincidentally, the results of the state test showed that Rhonda did not meet the state standards in reading.

Legal Issues

1. Discuss the appropriateness of Rhonda's placement in the regular classroom in these areas: academic benefit, nonacademic benefit, the effect of Rhonda on the regular classroom, and cost. In light of this discussion, discuss the least restrictive environment for Rhonda.
2. Given the information provided on accommodations and adaptations within the regular classroom, was Rhonda's IEP appropriate? Why or why not?
3. What are the possible legal consequences of Tranita Jackson's behavior?

Other Issues

1. Did Ms. Jackson make a good faith effort to carry out Rhonda's IEP? Did Ms. Mills make a good faith effort to carry out Rhonda's IEP? What evidence supports your answers?
2. What would be an appropriate way to resolve the conflict between the two teachers?

Activity

Work with a partner for this activity. Each person should assume the position of either Ms. Jackson (3rd-grade teacher) or Ms. Mills (special education teacher). Take a few minutes to think about that person's feelings and position on working with Rhonda. Now, with your partner, discuss your position. Try to listen to your partner without interrupting. Then state your position. Try to define and resolve the conflict.

CASE 8.2   Jameca

Major issue: Individualized education program (IEP)
Secondary issue: Free appropriate public education (FAPE)

Characters

Jameca Williams, 17-year-old boy with emotional disturbance

Belinda Williams, parent of Jameca

James Hudson, special education teacher

Jared Balm, special education administrator

"I've been stuck in special education classes since the 3rd grade, and I hate it! Once you get put into special education, you never get out. When people hear that I am 'BD,' they automatically think that I am a bad kid, and I'm not. I just get caught doing stupid things sometimes," said Jameca, a 17-year-old boy with emotional disturbance.

"That's right," said Belinda Williams, Jameca's mother. "I just hate the fact that Jameca is shoved into a cage every day at this school and doesn't get the same opportunities and education as all of the normal kids. In fact, I don't think Jameca is really 'BD'—I think he has a learning disability. I think the label 'BD' is a real problem. We realize that Jameca needs help in writing, reading, and math. If he was placed in the regular high school with extra help in these areas, his behavior would be just fine."

James Hudson, the special education teacher, watched and listened to Jameca and his mother as the other IEP team members sat around the conference table. Mr. Hudson knew Jameca quite well. Jameca was a student in his English and mathematics classes at Collins Treatment Center. Jameca had been a student at Collins for 2 years, and for 6 years prior to this placement had been in a self-contained class for students with emotional disturbance. Because of his experience with Jameca, it was clear to Mr. Hudson that the boy had a severe behavioral problem, and he decided to enter the discussion.

"Jameca," he began, "I hear you saying that you want to attend Wentzville High School. However, let me summarize my observations of your classroom behavior. Every day in class, you tell me that you don't have to listen to anybody, and I observe that you don't follow directions. Attendance is a major concern—but you recently told me that you don't have to come to class unless you want to. I have observed many dress code violations, like wearing baggy pants around your knees with a long shirt and a hat. I have observed disrespectful behavior directed toward students who are not Caucasian. Every day in class when you are here, you make frequent inappropriate remarks throughout the entire period. Both you and your mother want to see you placed into regular education classes full-time with resource assistance for help in reading, writing, and math—but I can assure you that the regular education high school teachers would not tolerate this behavior in their classrooms."

Ms. Williams quickly came to her son's defense by saying, "You are completely wrong about that, Mr. Hudson. Jameca does not have a behavior problem. I think it is your fault that he misbehaves. You provoke him. If you didn't force him to get to class on time, do his homework, and refrain from using inappropriate language, he would do just fine in school. Being in the BD program is ruining his life."

Jared Balm, special education administrator, who had been quietly listening up to this point, said, "Now, Ms. Williams, let's be reasonable. I know that you want Jameca to be successful and graduate from high school. We agree that we want him to move toward placement in the regular high school. However, we don't want to set him up for failure by sending him there before is ready. Let's review Jameca's behavioral goals."

Mr. Balm read the following goals from Jameca's completed IEP:

* Jameca will attend school 95% of the time. Any absence will be due to illness (evaluated by weekly review of attendance record and follow-up telephone conference with Ms. Williams to verify illness in case of absence).
* Jameca will be in his assigned seat for each class 95% of the time (evaluated by each teacher via observation on a weekly chart).
* Jameca will complete homework 4 of 5 days each week (evaluated by each teacher via observation on a weekly chart).
* Jameca will use appropriate language in the classroom—no foul language (evaluated by each teacher via observation on a weekly chart).
* Jameca will raise his hand in class to speak 95% of the time (evaluated by each teacher via observation on a weekly chart).
* Jameca will follow the dress code 100% of the time (evaluated by each teacher via observation on a weekly chart).
* Jameca will not use verbal "put downs" directed toward other students in class 95% of the time (evaluated by each teacher via observation on a weekly chart).

"Mr. Balm," said Mr. Hudson, "if Jameca could meet these goals over the next quarter, I think I could support a trial placement at the high school. I think that Jameca might have a chance at success if he earns the right to be at the regular high school. To earn this right, he would need to meet his goals."

Jameca slumped in his seat and nodded. His mother said, "I really want Jameca to be placed in the regular high school and I don't want him to be a 'BD' student. I also want you to stop provoking him and let him try to do what he's supposed to do. I am not too thrilled to wait, but I will agree—just as long as he gets the chance to make a change to the regular high school."

The remainder of the IEP meeting was spent reviewing Jameca's IEP. Part of the discussion included writing the Present Levels of Performance and specifying Jameca's placement in special education, as follows:

Present Levels of Performance

Student strengths: Jameca responds well to positive reinforcement and enjoys helping others. During the past year, Jameca read aloud to kindergarten students at an elementary school. Other students look up to Jameca.

How disability affects the student's involvement and progress in the general curriculum, including adverse effects of the disability: Jameca's inappropriate classroom behavior and his weak reading, writing, and mathematics skills affect his involvement in the general education curriculum. For example, Jameca can read independently at a 2nd-grade level, write a five-sentence paragraph with many spelling and mechanical errors, and can compute two-digit by two-digit addition and subtraction problems with carrying and regrouping. In addition, his overt behavior within the classroom is often inappropriate, including behaviors like not following teacher directions, telling the class that he doesn't have to listen to the teacher, talking out, using verbal "put-downs" directed toward African American students, not completing assigned tasks, and frequently not following the dress code. Jameca also displays poor school attendance and is often tardy to class. With the current academic skills and inappropriate behavior, Jameca would not be successful in the general education curriculum.

Parental concerns: Ms. Williams feels that Jameca belongs in the regular high school in general education classes with support for academic classes. She feels that Jameca's disability is a learning disability, not emotional disturbance.

Supplementary aids and services: Not applicable—Jameca does not at this time need accommodations in regular education classes or other education-related settings to enable him to be educated with nondisabled peers. However, he needs the following special classroom accommodations: extended time for test-taking, read test aloud to Jameca (except reading tests).

Participation in regular education classes and other education-related settings:
Regular Education, No Supplementary Aids: Not appropriate
Regular Education, with Supplementary Aids: Not appropriate

(*Continued*)

Special Education: Type—Emotional disturbance
                  Location—Public school day treatment facility
                  Amount/Frequency of Services—Full day/5 days per week
                  Initiation Date—Sept. 3
                  Duration of Services—May 31
Related Services: Type—Social work individual therapy
                  Location—Public school day treatment facility
                  Amount/Frequency of Services—60 minutes per day/5 days per week
                  Initiation Date—Sept. 3
                  Duration of Services—May 31

Extent to which the student will not participate with nondisabled students in regular education classes and extracurricular and other nonacademic activities:
__X__ Special Classes: Jameca will not participate in the regular education program for academic, nonacademic, or extracurricular classes or activities.
__X__ Separate Schooling: Jameca will not participate in the regular high school for academic, nonacademic, or extracurricular classes or activities.
__X__ Removal from the regular education environment is required because the nature or severity of the student's disability is such that education in regular classes with the use of supplementary aids and services cannot be achieved satisfactorily.

Placement Options Considered:
Regular high school with general education classes and resource assistance in special education.   Team Accepts Placement: _____ Yes __X__ No

Regular high school with special education classes.
Team Accepts Placement: _____ Yes __X__ No

Public school special education day treatment facility.
Team Accepts Placement: __X__ Yes _____ No

       After the meeting, Mr. Hudson was relieved. He agreed with Jameca and his mother that many children, once classified as emotionally disturbed, do not get out of the system. However, in this case, he recognized that Jameca was already in the least restrictive environment—it would be hard work for Jameca to make it to the regular high school and even more work for him to stay there. Sometimes children are mislabeled—and by doing so, they may suffer from social stigmas—but in this instance, Mr. Hudson didn't think the system had failed the student.
       End note: One month after this IEP meeting, Jameca cursed the teacher and walked out of school, never to return. At 17 years of age, he dropped out of school.

Legal Issues

1. How does IDEA address least restrictive environment?
2. According to the information provided, was Jameca placed in the least restrictive environment? What evidence leads you to this conclusion?
3. Was Jameca's IEP individualized to meet his special needs? How do you know?

Other Issues

1. Should the team have placed Jameca in the regular high school on a trial basis? Why or why not?
2. What could the team have done to prevent Jameca from dropping out of school?

Activity

Review the parts of Jameca's IEP that are presented and review his goals. Revise it so that Jameca would be more successful in school. Be sure to add transition services. Funding should not be considered a barrier.

Chapter **9**

Due Process

CASE 9.1   Darnell

Major issue: Discipline

Secondary issue: Free appropriate public education (FAPE)

Characters

Latrina Duffin, parent

Darnell Duffin, 5th-grade child with learning disability

John Rhoads, attorney for parent

Lynn Gleason, principal

"This should never have happened," Latrina Duffin tearfully said to John Rhoads, her attorney. "They took my baby out of school, to jail—and made him clean toilets!"

Mr. Rhoads said, "I know you are very upset, Ms. Duffin, but let's start at the beginning. Please tell me exactly what happened."

Ms. Duffin regained her composure and then told her story: "I received a telephone call on March 10 in the afternoon from Ms. Gleason, the principal. She told me that Darnell was disruptive. He was already gone when she called me. They took him away in a police car and the police didn't call me or anything. They didn't even ask my permission to remove Darnell from school property! I don't remember seeing this in the school handbook—that they will use this kind of discipline. I picked up Darnell at the police station and he said he was scared and thought they were taking him to jail. Then they made him clean toilets and mop floors! Darnell has a learning disability and is not a bad kid. He just learns at a slow pace and gets frustrated. They keep trying to tear down his character. The principal told me Darnell wouldn't look at her when she was talking to him, so she punished him by calling the police. Darnell has had panic attacks and nightmares since this incident. The principal suspended him after this happened, then told me at an IEP meeting that he couldn't come back to school this year. She said that the school would provide tutoring at home, but the tutor has only been to my house one time. This whole incident is just abuse by the school district."

Mr. Rhoads took detailed notes as Ms. Duffin talked. He then asked clarifying questions about the incident. Ms. Duffin handed him a 4-inch-thick stack of school records. Mr. Rhoads assured Ms. Duffin that he would take the case. After reviewing the records, he drafted a letter to the school district requesting a due process hearing. After both parties agreed to waive a resolution meeting and the school district would not agree to mediation, the date for the hearing was set and preparations were made for prospective witnesses.

The due process hearing was held in the school district conference room at 9 a.m. on April 11. Part of the direct examination of Lynn Gleason, principal, by John Rhoads, attorney for the parent, follows.

Mr. Rhoads: Ms. Gleason, would you please state your full name, your relationship to Darnell, and your qualifications for the record?

Ms. Gleason: Yes, my name is Lynn Gleason, and I am the principal of Lincoln Elementary School, where Darnell attends school. I have been a principal for 5 years and I have a bachelor's degree in elementary education with a master's degree in educational administration. I am certified to teach elementary grades through 6th grade and to be a building principal at the elementary, middle, and high school levels.

Mr. Rhoads: Ms. Gleason, how many times has Darnell been suspended this school year and for what offenses?

Ms. Gleason: Darnell has been very disruptive in school. He constantly disrupts the learning process. And . . .

Mr. Rhoads: Ms. Gleason, how many times has Darnell been suspended this year?

Ms. Gleason: I think about 26 times.

Mr. Rhoads: And how many days has Darnell been out of school as a result of the suspensions?

Ms. Gleason: About 30 days.

Mr. Rhoads: Please tell us what Darnell did to deserve suspensions totaling 30 school days.

Ms. Gleason (as she flips through suspension notices): I'll just read these to you—Eating candy in class after being told to stop . . . engaging in verbal wordplay with other student in the classroom . . . pushing another student on the playground . . . talking back to the teacher . . . throwing books in the classroom . . . refusing to complete assignments . . .

(Ms. Gleason reads the complete list.)

Mr. Rhoads: Ms. Gleason, are you aware that Darnell has a disability and is placed in a special education classroom for the majority of his school day?

Ms. Gleason: Yes, of course. I attended several IEP meetings on Darnell, and I know that he has a learning disability.

Mr. Rhoads: Ms. Gleason, would you read the present levels of performance on Darnell's IEP?

Ms. Gleason (reading): Darnell has attention deficit hyperactivity disorder, resulting in impulsive and inattentive behavior. He sometimes does not follow adult instructions and talks out of turn in class. In addition, Darnell functions approximately 3 years below grade level in reading, writing, and mathematics. He has difficulty sounding out words using phonetic skills, but can write simple sentences, although spelling is usually incorrect. He can solve 2-digit by 2-digit addition and subtraction problems, but is unable to remember multiplication facts to 10.

Mr. Rhoads: Thank you. Now, were you present when Darnell's behavior management plan was written to address his behavior?

Ms. Gleason: No, I was out of the building that day, but I am aware of the plan.

Mr. Rhoads: Were you present at the manifestation determination meeting held on February 25?

Ms. Gleason: Yes, I was present and I agreed that Darnell's behavior was related to his disability.

Mr. Rhoads: Ms. Gleason, tell me what you understand to be the rule about suspension of a child with a disability.

Ms. Gleason: I don't know about a rule, but I always thought a child could be suspended 10 days. However, if a child continually misbehaves, I feel that I have the right to protect the learning environment for other children in the building. I don't think I did anything wrong.

Mr. Rhoads: Ms. Gleason, please tell us what happened on the day of the behavior incident when the police were contacted.

Ms. Gleason: Darnell was sent to my office from his classroom with a note that he was making fun of another student during reading class. I talked to Darnell, and he laughed at me. I then told him to look at me when I talked to him. He blatantly refused. I was very angry with Darnell, and I decided to take an extreme measure by contacting the police. I asked Lt. Howard Eads to come to the building and try to teach Darnell a lesson in how to behave. We have an informal agreement with Lt. Eads that if I make a request, he will take the child to the police department for an "in-station adjustment" program. Part of the in-station adjustment is to require the student to perform community service. The community service in Darnell's case was to clean some toilets and mop the floor. I thought this would teach Darnell a good lesson because nothing I did in the building was making any difference.

Legal Issues

1. List legal errors on the part of the school district and tell why each is an error.

2. Describe the process of the due process hearing. Tell what happened first, second, and so forth. Did the district follow the correct legal process from the information given?

3. Describe the strategy used by Mr. Rhoads when questioning Ms. Gleason. Why do you think he asked these particular questions?

Other Issues

1. Is it appropriate for the police to become involved in this case? Why or why not? In what circumstances should the police become involved in the discipline of the school?

2. Describe what could have been done to avoid this due process hearing.

Activity

You are Darnell's special education teacher and are very frustrated with Darnell's behavior as described in the due process hearing. Develop an appropriate behavioral intervention plan (BIP) for Darnell that would target specific undesirable behaviors and avoid excessive suspensions from school.

CASE 9.2   Andrew

Major issue: Individualized education program (IEP)
Secondary issue: Free appropriate public education (FAPE)

Characters

Andrew Stephens, kindergarten child

Andrea Stephens, mother

John Stephens, father

George Collins, special education director

Ms. Cindy Potter, early childhood special education teacher

Ms. Tucker, special education teacher

Judy Miles, kindergarten teacher

Jennifer McKinney, parent attorney

Lynn Grayton, principal

Andrea Stephens:

I walked into the school office 2 days after Andrew's IEP meeting. I asked to speak with Ms. Grayton, the principal. I inquired about the next IEP meeting, which was to be held at 8 a.m. the following week. My husband and I were supposed to make two classroom observations of potential placements for Andrew prior to the next meeting. I told Ms. Grayton that my husband and I already made the observations and were ready to finalize the date of the IEP meeting. What she said startled me.

Ms. Grayton said, "Ms. Stephens, you must have misunderstood."

I said, "What do you mean, 'misunderstood'? We agreed 2 days ago in Andrew's IEP meeting that we would meet next week to finalize his placement change. You attended the meeting and you agreed."

Ms. Grayton said, "No, we did not agree to hold a meeting next week. In fact, I'm not completely sure how quickly we can hold another meeting. I need to schedule the meeting through the special education office. We may need to talk again to discuss placement alternatives."

I was furious! I *know* that we agreed Andrew would move to a more appropriate educational setting. *Everyone* at the meeting agreed that he needed additional support. What happened? I talked with my husband and we decided to engage an attorney, Jennifer McKinney. We immediately

93

contacted her and were advised to write a due process complaint. We spent the majority of the evening drafting the letter. The next day, I took the letter and hand-delivered it to the director of special education and the superintendent. The letter read as follows:

September 10

Mr. George Collins
Director of Special Education
105 Bluff Street
Reedville

Parents: Andrea and John Stephens
Child: Andrew Stephens
Address: 230 Julia Place
                Reedville
School: Lincoln Elementary

Dear Mr. Collins:

Request
Because of my concerns about the appropriate placement of my son, Andrew, I have been advised to write a letter detailing the problems with his current placement, options for a resolution, and a time line for a response from the district regarding my request. Hopefully, this can be resolved quickly without the intervention of attorneys. If you are unwilling to grant my request, please consider this letter as a request for a due process hearing. I will be represented by Ms. Jennifer McKinney. Please send a complete copy of Andrew's file to Ms. McKinney at McKinney Law Firm, 7 Main St., Reedville, Iowa.

IEP Meetings—May 1 and May 10
On May 1, I met with you and your staff at the annual IEP meeting to discuss an appropriate education program for my son, Andrew. At this meeting, you told me that Andrew no longer qualified for the early childhood special education program. When I asked why he no longer qualified, you told me: (1) he had turned 5 years old, (2) he had met all of his IEP goals for the year, and (3) he demonstrated some abilities on a kindergarten checklist. You had no norm-referenced tests or data to support this recommendation. At that time, I expressed concerns about the proposed placement of kindergarten for the next year. I reminded the team that children are required to begin kindergarten no later than the age of 6, *not* 5. It is

also common practice in this school district for children to remain in early childhood until age 6.

I was told that Andrew had less intensive needs than many of the children in early childhood, and that he needed a less restrictive environment. I agreed that he needed more inclusion with children who did not have disabilities, but I questioned the wisdom of "dumping" him into a general education class without a transition period. He would virtually be going from a classroom of eight children, one teacher, and four paraprofessionals to a class of 20 to 25 children and one teacher. I was told that Andrew's transition period would be during the last 2 weeks of school when he would be integrated into the prekindergarten class. I didn't consider this an appropriate transition time period or placement.

The team recommended that Andrew's placement for the following year be in the general education kindergarten classroom with 20 minutes of speech-language services 4 days a week. You told me that special education services did not appear necessary, and the speech-language therapist would be best suited to work with the kindergarten teacher to address his needs in the classroom. I expressed my concern that Andrew's language disability would impact his ability to perform independently in a general education classroom. I stated that Andrew had made great progress, and that he was closing the gap between his language skills and those of his peers, but that he still continued to have difficulty with language skills that allow him to be able to function independently in larger group settings with children his own age. I explained my personal experiences with Andrew, in out-of-school activities, and his inability to successfully interact with children his own age. I told the team that he functioned much better with children a year younger than himself. Although Andrew had some of the academic skills required in kindergarten, he by no means had the language skills that were necessary. I expressed my concern that Andrew would become frustrated in a kindergarten environment without comprehensive support, where he would be unable to understand the majority of the language. I predicted that he would either withdraw or act out. I was told that there was always the ability to have Andrew repeat kindergarten.

The team disagreed with me. I was very upset and told the team that I believed they were going to let Andrew fail. You told me that we could reevaluate this placement after the first 4 weeks of the school year. I did not sign the IEP and left the meeting.

On May 4, I called Ms. Potter, Andrew's early childhood special education teacher, to inform her that I disagreed with the change of placement. I then called you to inform you of this decision. On the phone, I told you I did not agree that the kindergarten placement was sufficient to meet Andrew's needs. You told me that my request—placing Andrew in special education for consultation—would take up a place on that teacher's caseload. I told you that this decision was *not* based on the teacher's caseload—it *was* based on a free appropriate education for my son, Andrew. I told you I would pursue legal action if Andrew was not at least placed on consultation in special education for the following year. You told me you would contact the teacher about setting up another IEP meeting. On May 6, Ms. Potter called me to reschedule an IEP meeting.

On May 10, I met with your staff to rewrite Andrew's IEP. This IEP changed Andrew's placement for the upcoming school year in kindergarten to include 20 minutes of speech-language pull-out services 4 days a week, and 30 minutes of special education consultation weekly. I again expressed my concern about moving Andrew to kindergarten, but agreed to rely on the opinion of the team. I was told that Ms. Miles would be the kindergarten teacher and that the IEP would be reviewed after the first 4 weeks of school.

Chronology—Kindergarten

On August 19, Andrew started kindergarten at Lincoln School in Ms. Miles's class. The first day was a half-day. Andrew came home from school in tears. He said he had "got a red card at school and had to talk to the principal." He said the principal was "disappointed with me." I told my husband that it was impossible for Andrew to get a red card on the first day of kindergarten, and immediately called the teacher. Ms. Miles reported that Andrew had been very good during the day, but he was asked to keep his feet still by a helper in the classroom during story time. The helper had long blond hair and looked like the principal. Ms. Miles said they had talked about the behavior cards and explained that if you get in big trouble you will get a red card and have to go the principal's office. Andrew had been confused. He thought that if he was disciplined at all he was in "big trouble," and he thought the helper *was* the principal. During his 2 years in early childhood, Andrew was *never* in trouble. Therefore, he was very upset. He didn't want to go back to school. He said he didn't belong there.

On August 22, I talked to Ms. Miles because the classroom helper may have told Andrew she was disappointed with him and he was upset. The helper was in the room and she stated that she never told Andrew she was disappointed with him. She talked to Andrew and told him that he wasn't in trouble. Ms. Miles told me that she had 24 children in her room and that she was doing her best to address

Andrew's needs. She told me she would try to explain things individually to Andrew.

On August 25, Ms. Miles e-mailed to tell me that Andrew lost his lunch recess, because he was talking too loudly in the cafeteria. Ms. Miles said Andrew was easily influenced by another student's misbehavior. Andrew told me later that another boy was poking him and calling him "stupid." When he was telling the other boy to stop, he got in trouble for talking too loudly. He was unable to explain the situation to the cafeteria helper. After a second warning, he lost his recess.

On August 26, Andrew began to spontaneously "write" letters to Ms. Miles telling her he was going back to Ms. Potter's room (his early childhood teacher). He began having bad dreams and crying in his sleep. He started complaining that he was sick and couldn't go to school. He told me that "everybody doesn't like me at school," "I not good at kindergarten," "kindergarten is too hard for me cause I don't have the real word."

On August 30, Andrew reported that he lost lunch recess again for talking too loudly.

On September 1, before school, I talked to Ms. Miles about recess. She reported that Andrew had a hard time focusing in class. Ms. Miles told me that the required kindergarten speech-language screening with Andrew was completed and that he had a lot of difficulty and needed several breaks to complete the screening.

Andrew came home from school very upset on September 2. He lost his lunch recess again and had been pushed into the bathroom wall by another student. He went to the office to see the nurse for the bump he received from the incident and begged not to go back to school by saying, "Please call Mommy, I all done kindergarten, okay?"

On September 3, I requested an observation by one of my colleagues, a school psychologist. I arranged the observation so that suggestions could be offered on how to address Andrew's needs in the upcoming IEP review. I left the message for the principal with the school secretary.

On September 5, I talked to Ms. Miles and the speech-language therapist. Both teachers said they would welcome an outside observation. Ms. Miles noted that she could see Andrew's frustration at school and that he seemed to have a lot of difficulty keeping up with the class and following more than a one-step direction. She commented that Andrew often appeared "sad." She also said that she would appreciate additional strategies to help Andrew. I also asked about the upcoming IEP meeting. I was told that meetings were set for September 13 and I was given a list of times from which to choose. I went to the office to ask the principal about the observation.

She was out of the building, so I called her later that day. I was told that she would have to check with the special education director before she could agree to an outside observation. On this day, Andrew got in trouble for pushing. Later that day, he was sent to the office complaining that his "brain hurt."

On September 8, the principal called and informed me that the request for an observation was denied. She explained she wanted to give Andrew more time to adjust to school. Ms. Miles e-mailed to say that Andrew was able to "keep his green card" today, but he continued to have trouble focusing and participating at group times.

On September 10, Andrew lost his green card again at school. He continued to have difficulty following directions.

Ms. Miles told me on September 14 that Andrew had started masturbating in class. I was told by a child psychologist that this behavior was a reaction to stress.

At this point, I was beginning to see a pattern of behavior in Andrew. He cried easily at home, complained that he was sick, begged to stay home each day, and acted out at school. He had more disciplinary actions taken against him in the short time he was in kindergarten than he had in the previous 2 years of school. He was verbalizing his dislike for school, saying "it's too hard," "they use big word," "I'm not good at kindergarten," "I don't do things right," and "I hate school."

I then called the superintendent. You [special education director] returned my phone call and said you had heard that I'd been calling the district. I told you I was upset because the district wasn't following through on the agreed-upon plan. You told me that you didn't think the team had agreed to a meeting for the following week, and you were looking at options. You said you didn't think there was agreement to change Andrew's placement. I said you couldn't know this since you weren't at the meeting. At one point in the conversation, you wanted to "brainstorm" possible solutions and suggested kindergarten half-day and early childhood special education half-day. This was very confusing for me because if you wanted to brainstorm, you could have attended the IEP meeting. You even suggested that you were trying to help Andrew. If so, why would you wait until after the IEP meeting to order an observation by a school psychologist, when I had requested one 2 weeks earlier by an outside consultant? This seemed very late, considering that *you* were the person who suggested the IEP review after the first 4 weeks of school, and you and your staff were *very* aware of my concerns about the kindergarten placement. Last year, you told me that the team would be able to "move quickly" if it was determined that the placement was not working. That is exactly what happened at the IEP meeting. I expected you to follow through with the team's suggestions and recommendations, even if you did not attend the meeting. According to IDEA, the *team* makes placement decisions. Once those decisions have been made, you are legally responsible for following through.

IEP Meeting—September 18

I attended the IEP on September 18, along with a parent advocate. At the meeting, the kindergarten teacher, speech therapist, and special education teacher took turns discussing Andrew's difficulties at school. No one presented any information that supported the idea that this placement was appropriate for Andrew. In fact, the only positive comments I heard focused on Andrew's cooperative, compliant nature, and his desire to do well at school. The teachers discussed his difficulty keeping up with the group, following directions, listening, paying attention, and understanding what to do. One teacher commented that he displayed frustration and appeared sad. It was also stated that he was very upset when he lost his green card. I made it clear that I believed Andrew needed an immediate change of placement. I presented the outside testing conducted by a private speech-language clinic. The scores showed continued expressive and receptive language delays and an overall functional level in language of 4.0 to 4.5 age level. The clinician also reported that the language in kindergarten was challenging for Andrew and a prekindergarten placement might be the most appropriate placement. I also reported that the scores showed he was making progress. I reported that Andrew came home from school every day disappointed. He was expressing his frustration and dislike for school every day. He was begging to stay home or go back to the early childhood classroom. I told the team that Andrew was just hanging on by a thread and that his behavior would become disruptive. Right now he was compliant, but that wouldn't continue if he didn't begin to feel some measure of success. The principal began a discussion on adding additional minutes to Andrew's current special education placement in Ms. Tucker's room and more support from an aide in the kindergarten room. The team discussed the need for growing independence in kindergarten and how the language and academic demands would increase. They talked about how much difficulty Andrew was having and how he couldn't cope with more demands. This suggestion was rejected by the team. Then Ms. Grayton, the principal, suggested the kindergarten–1st grade special education class at another school. I said that I had considered that class, so she requested that I observe in the classroom. I requested to arrange another IEP meeting for the following week or to have the team agree to a placement of either prekindergarten or the kindergarten–1st grade special classroom immediately, because Andrew just couldn't go on much longer. One team member said she had a meeting on Tuesday of the next week at 8:00, but she could meet any other morning. The rest of the team said they could meet at 8:00 on any morning except Tuesday. I again asked to set the meeting for the next week. Ms. Grayton told me that after I observed at the other school, I could come to her office, and we would set the IEP meeting for a morning the following week.

Although Andrew made tremendous progress in the early childhood special education program, it is evident that the current placement in kindergarten with special education consultation and 20 minutes of speech-language therapy four days a week is not the appropriate placement to meet his needs.

Solution
As a conscientious parent (and member of the IEP team who agreed that Andrew needs a change of placement), I cannot agree to continue with the current placement. Andrew's needs are not being met. After careful consideration and observation of other classrooms, I believe the only appropriate placement for Andrew is in the early childhood special education program with integration in the prekindergarten classroom for the majority of the day. This would be a continuation of the successful placement from the last school year. This would *truly* give Andrew the transition period necessary to be successful in general education kindergarten the following year.

Because Andrew is guaranteed the right to a free *appropriate* public education under IDEA, it is critical to address this situation quickly. I was told at the IEP meeting that we would meet this week to consider "placement determination." I have been extremely patient with this process and have done my best to make the personnel in the district aware of my concerns. Therefore, I would like an IEP meeting and a response to my request for a change of placement by Friday.

Thank you for your consideration. I look forward to hearing from you.

Sincerely,

Ms. Andrea Stephens, parent

Cc: Superintendent

Legal Issues

1. What must be included in a due process complaint? Did this letter meet the requirements?
2. What are the next steps in the legal process of resolving this complaint? Who is responsible for the next steps?
3. How could this conflict have been resolved before it escalated into a request for a due process hearing?

Other Issues

1. Review Figure 1.8 from chapter 1—"Principles of Least Restrictive Environment." Discuss the extent to which each principle was followed.
2. What do you think will be the outcome of this case? What evidence supports your hypothesis?

Activity

Dispositions are attitudes that professionals display in their interactions with parents and students. Appropriate dispositions are essential to successful interactions and collaboration. Choose two of the following characters from this case: Mr. Collins, special education director; Ms. Miles, kindergarten teacher; Ms. Grayton, principal. In a small group discussion, answer the following questions using examples from this case as evidence:

1. To what extent did this character show respect for diversity and tolerance for others?
2. To what extent did this character show a willingness to collaborate and learn from others?
3. To what extent did this character have the ability to look at situations from others' points of view?
4. To what extent did this character demonstrate sound ethical judgment?
5. To what extent did this character demonstrate motivation to work with students who displayed a variety of needs?
6. To what extent did this character demonstrate the capability to advocate for students with disabilities?
7. How did the dispositions of one character differ from the other character discussed?

Chapter **10**

Parent Participation

CASE 10.1 **Dan**

Major issue: Individualized education program (IEP)
Secondary issue: Free appropriate public education (FAPE)

Characters

Dan Peterson, 3rd-grade child with learning disability

Valorie Peterson, parent

Tony Wells, school psychologist

Jana Branson, principal

Jackie Smith, special education teacher

Lee Craft, 3rd-grade teacher

Valorie Peterson:
Wouldn't it be terrific if parents could look forward to their child's IEP meeting? Wouldn't it be great if parents could go into these meetings knowing that they would walk out feeling good, proud, and satisfied? However, as I thought about Dan's recent IEP meeting, I felt knots form in my stomach. Several things distinguished the meeting: There were too many people in the room and each pushed for his or her own agenda. The meeting focused on evaluations and what Dan could *not* do. Then I remember feeling sick. Then the professionals told me what goals they had for Dan and how they were going to "fix" his problems.

　　Dan was first made eligible for special education services as a student with a learning disability this year, in 3rd grade. Dan quickly fell behind in reading at the beginning of 3rd grade and the teacher suggested an evaluation for special education. Although I was upset at the thought of Dan having a disability, I simply could not allow him to continue with the frustration he felt every day during school. Dan often came home crying with 3 hours of homework. It was just too much for him to keep up with the class. Therefore, I agreed to an evaluation. I wasn't completely sure what to expect, but I gave written consent for the evaluation. Three weeks later, I received a formal notice in the mail scheduling an IEP meeting to discuss the results of the evaluation.

I walked into the meeting with some reservations, but hopeful that Dan might receive some extra help in reading. The room was full of people I had never met. Before the meeting began, Ms. Branson, the principal, entered the room in a hurry. She stated that she was too busy to attend the meeting because she had to meet the school buses as they arrived. She asked to sign her name to a document, and then quickly exited. After some brief introductions, the school psychologist, Mr. Wells, began to discuss Dan's test results. He read from a prepared report and talked quickly. I tried to listen, but I was not familiar with the terms he used: *IQ, general achievement, discrepancy, gap between ability and achievement, difficulty with phonemic awareness.* Then Mr. Wells looked up from his report and told me that Dan had a learning disability and was eligible for special education services. Everyone else in the meeting nodded in agreement. I said, "Does this mean that Dan will get an after-school tutor?" Mr. Wells quickly said, "No, but let me show you what kind of services Dan *will* receive." Then another teacher, Ms. Smith, who was the special education teacher, took out a multipage document that was already completely filled out. She began to review the document with me. It included terms that I had never heard before, like *present levels of performance, goals, special education services,* and *accommodations.* Again I asked, "Will Dan receive extra help in reading?"

Ms. Smith pointed to a section of the document and said, "Yes, Dan will receive 30 minutes of reading instruction from me every day. I will work with Dan in a small group of children so that I can give him individual assistance. He will be taken out of the 3rd-grade classroom during his reading time. I will also provide extra help with social studies and science."

I wasn't quite sure what to say, but I wanted Dan to receive help in reading. Before I could respond, Ms. Smith continued, "Here are the goals I have for Dan. These goals are the same as for all of my 3rd-grade students. The first goal says: 'Dan will increase reading skills by one year.' The second goal says: 'Dan will be able to read a story at the 2nd-grade level and answer comprehension question.' I really think Dan will benefit from my program. We recently purchased a new reading series in special education and Dan will fit nicely in the program and in the group of children I work with."

Ms. Craft, Dan's 3rd-grade teacher, followed with additional comments: "Ms. Peterson, Dan is failing reading at this time in my classroom. In my reading class, Dan must be able to read a novel, like *Little House in the Big Woods,* which is written on a 5th-grade level, and complete many detailed comprehension worksheets on each chapter. He simply can't keep up. I know that you've seen him come home with a considerable amount of homework daily. If he stays in my class, he will probably get an F on his report card."

Again, it was difficult for me to respond. I was choked with emotion. I knew that Dan was struggling in reading, but now I was being told that Dan would fail reading unless he left the classroom for special education assistance. I wanted Dan to get help, but I was somewhat uneasy with him being singled out to go to a special education classroom. Dan was very sensitive and would be self-conscious walking out of the room. However, I didn't say anything about his emotional status. I said that I wanted him to pass reading class and learn to read.

Mr. Wells stated, "Good. Then we are all in agreement with the plan. Ms. Peterson, we will need your signature right here on this form for Dan to receive special help in reading. He can begin next Monday if you sign now." Mr. Wells placed a form in front of me.

What choice did I have? I barely glanced at the form, and then signed it. Everyone looked happy and began to get up from the table. Mr. Wells stayed behind and gave me copies of Dan's IEP, the conference report, and the permission form. I had the distinct feeling that this group of professionals had conducted this meeting in advance. There was really very little discussion about what Dan could and could not do except for the brief summary of the psychologist's test results. I felt that the group had previously discussed Dan prior to the meeting. It seemed that they already knew what was going to happen before it occurred.

Looking back, I only wish that I could have had an idea of what was going to be discussed. I would have appreciated having the same information as the other team members prior to the meeting, so that I could have reviewed the information myself. In reflecting on the meeting, I wonder why the team focused on Dan's weaknesses and focused so little on his strengths and his positive attributes. Nothing positive was stated about Dan. However, I felt that I had to go along with the team's recommendations to get extra help for Dan.

Legal Issues

1. To what extent were the following legal guidelines followed in the development of Dan's IEP?
   * Informed parental consent for initial placement in special education.
   * IEP team consideration of the concerns of the parents for enhancing the education of their child.
   * Assurance by the school district that parents of a child with a disability are members of any group that makes decisions on the educational placement of their child.

2. To what extent was Dan's IEP individualized to meet his needs?

3. Legally, who should be involved in an IEP team meeting? Were the appropriate people involved in Dan's IEP meeting?

Other Issues

1. Do you agree with Ms. Peterson that the group of professionals had conducted the IEP meeting in advance? Why or why not? If the team had made determinations prior to the meeting, could this become a legal concern? Why or why not?
2. Would it have been appropriate to send Ms. Peterson information (e.g., psychological report, draft IEP, teacher observation report) prior to the IEP meeting? Why or why not?

Activity

You are Dan's special education teacher and are in attendance at the IEP meeting described in this case. Determine four places where Ms. Peterson could have been more involved in the IEP process. Write four questions and/or actions directed toward Ms. Peterson that might have increased meaningful participation. The chart below might help you structure the questions and/or actions.

Place during the IEP meeting where Ms. Peterson could have been more involved	Potential questions and/or actions to elicit meaningful participation
Example: The room where the IEP meeting was held was full of people the parent had never met. After some brief introductions . . .	*Example:* Each participant would write his or her name on a nametag and wear the tag. During introductions, each participant would tell how he or she is involved in Dan's education and make one strength-based statement about what Dan can do.

CASE 10.2 Maria

Major issue: Individualized education program (IEP)
Secondary issue: Free appropriate public education (FAPE)

Characters

    Maria Kolchenko, kindergarten child with a disability

    Kate Kolchenko, parent of Maria

    Max Feldon, school social worker

Ms. Kolchenko picked up the telephone as it rang a second time and said, "Hello."

    "Ms. Kolchenko? This is Max Feldon, the school social worker. I called to talk with you about Maria's progress."

    Ms. Kolchenko, not expecting this phone call, answered, "Yes, Mr. Feldon, what do you want to discuss?"

    Mr. Feldon stated, "Ms. Kolchenko, as you know, I was unable to attend Maria's recent IEP meeting 3 weeks ago because I was out of the district on that day. I know the IEP team decided to keep Maria in the regular education kindergarten with support from the special education teacher, an individual aide, speech-language services, and the services of the social worker. After working with Maria for 3 weeks, I really don't think she needs the intensity of services planned. In addition, since I am only in the building one day a week, it is almost impossible to schedule Maria for the services."

    Ms. Kolchenko was surprised. "That's interesting," she said.

    Mr. Feldon continued, "Maria is supposed to receive individual pull-out services on a weekly basis for the whole year, and I'm also supposed to work with her every week on an individual basis in the kindergarten classroom for the entire year. In addition, she comes with a group of kindergarten students to see me weekly for the entire school year. This, I think, is not necessary and there is no way I can schedule all these services for one child. I really don't think it is necessary for Maria to see me three different times each week."

    Ms. Kolchenko was feeling upset as she said, "Mr. Feldon, do you have data to demonstrate that Maria does not need the social work services to the extent planned by the IEP team?"

Ms. Feldon answered, "Well, no, not exactly. I don't keep that kind of data, but based on my professional opinion, Maria just doesn't need the services."

Ms. Kolchenko said, "Mr. Feldon, please give me the data to show that Maria does not need the services, and then we can talk about changing services, at the annual review that will be scheduled in the spring."

The conversation ended quickly and Ms. Kolchenko was upset, but decided not to pursue the issue with the school because an IEP meeting had not been held or scheduled. She decided that the social worker might have been having a frustrating day. Just yesterday, Maria came home excited about her visit from Mr. Feldon in the kindergarten classroom.

The next day, Ms. Kolchenko received the following conference summary from Mr. Feldon:

Conference Summary
Conference date: October 10

Student: Maria Kolchenko   Birth date: March 6
Parent's name: Ms. Kate Kolchenko   Grade: Kindergarten
Address: 105 Bluff Drive

Current placement: Special Education Resource

Conference participants: Ms. Kolchenko, parent; Mr. Feldon, social worker

Purpose of conference: Phone contact to address the initiation and duration dates of the social work minutes in the IEP

Summary:
In a phone conference with Ms. Kolchenko, the decision was made to change the initiation and duration dates of the social work minutes on Maria's IEP. The dates should read as follows:
Social work direct individual pull-out: 20 minutes per session for 16 sessions; initiation 9/23 to 1/9
Social work group pull-out: 20 minutes per session at 27 sessions; initiation 9/23 to 5/5
Social work group push-in: 20 minutes at 15 sessions; initiation 1/9 to 5/5
Completed by: Max Feldon, school social worker

Ms. Kolchenko was furious! Just 3 weeks ago, an IEP team determined that Maria needed social work services along with speech and language services, an individual aide, and special education resource services. Everyone at the meeting agreed and an IEP was written. Ms. Kolchenko wondered how the social worker could change an IEP based on an informal telephone conversation. She thought that the parent was supposed to have input into the decisions. Why were the services included in the IEP 3 weeks ago now being withdrawn? In addition, didn't the social worker have to show data to substantiate a decision to take services away from Maria? How could there be data in just 3 weeks?

Ms. Kolchenko talked with her husband about the situation and they agreed that a letter should be written to the school district. Ms. Kolchenko drafted a letter and sent it to school the next day, with a copy to other administrators in the district.

October 22

Dear Mr. Feldon,

After receiving the Conference Summary you sent home with Maria, I have some questions. You told me that you are only available at the school one day a week and that it is difficult to schedule 60 minutes of social work services on that limited schedule. However, there was an abundance of data presented at the IEP meeting held in September to document Maria's needs for individual, small group, and push-in social work services. In lieu of any data that you have contrary to that presented at the meeting in September, I would feel uncomfortable withdrawing services at this time. I feel it is especially important to maintain the push-in services since it is Maria's least restrictive environment. Therefore, I do not agree to your proposed changes.

Additionally, I don't feel our impromptu phone conversation could be considered a conference to address initiation and duration of social work services. Maria enjoys working with you and I feel that you are making a positive impact on her ability to be integrated into the kindergarten classroom. Thanks for your hard work!

Sincerely,

Ms. Kate Kolchenko

Cc: Principal; Special Education Administrator; Superintendent

Legal Issues

1. According to IDEA, describe the procedures for changing an IEP. To what extent did this social worker follow those procedures?
2. Discuss the legal foundation of withdrawing services based on the provider's schedule. Why is this a problematic issue?

Other Issues

1. To what extent should the parent have been involved in this proposed IEP change?
2. What should the parent do if the district makes the change—that is, discontinues some of the social work services?

Activity

You are the special education administrator of this school district and you just received a copy of the letter from Ms. Kolchenko.

1. List the actions you would take to investigate the issue.
2. Tell how you would resolve the conflict.
3. Draft a letter to Ms. Kolchenko telling her how the issue could be resolved.

Appendix **A**

Matrix of Important Issues Used in Case Studies

Issues	Chapter/Case																	
	2.1	2.2	3.1	3.2	4.1	4.2	5.1	5.2	6.1	6.2	7.1	7.2	8.1	8.2	9.1	9.2	10.1	10.2
IEP	★											■	★	★		★	★	★
State assessment		★	★	★		★			■									
Response to intervention					★					■								
Discipline							★	★							★			
Accommodations		■							★					■				
Eligibility					■	■	■			★								
Transition				■				■			★							
FAPE	■	■									■	★		■	■	■	■	■

★Major issue

■Secondary issue

Appendix **B**

A Guide for Analyzing the Cases

The intent of this casebook is to provide a bridge between legal knowledge of special education law and application of this knowledge to the "real world." To assist the instructor and students in guiding discussion, a cognitive map for each case is included. The intent of the cognitive map is not to provide answers for students, but to assist in guiding discussion of important legal issues and other issues raised. As students discuss the issues listed in the cognitive map, they are better able to answer questions. Also included is a framework of professional dispositions—that is, attitudes—that often affects the foundation of legal issues and other issues raised in cases. This framework is the same for all cases and may be used to enrich the student's understanding of issues in the cases. In addition, there is a list of key terms so that students can focus on key ideas. For some cases, important foundation information is listed as optional "homework" for students. This "homework" may be assigned as extra research on issues raised in the case.

To use each case, it is suggested that the following procedure be followed:

1. Place students in small learning groups to read the cases.
2. Ask each group to list the important legal issues raised in each case and other issues raised in each case, then to answer the questions posed at the end of the case. Listing important issues will help students focus on answers to the questions.
3. After small group discussion, the class should discuss legal issues and other issues raised in the case. Then discuss answers to the questions posed at the end of each case. The optional activity may then be completed.

Cognitive Map to Guide Discussion
Chapter 2, Case 2.1: Brandon

Important Legal Issues Raised	Other Issues Raised
Connection of IEP goals to assessment	Grades as a reflection of academic progress
Method of assessing progress toward IEP goals	Use of general standardized achievement test to track academic progress
Components of IEP	

Discussion—Foundation of Legal Issues and Other Issues Raised—Consider the Professional's:

Effective communication skills—verbal and written

Ability to self-reflect

Ability and willingness to collaborate with families and other professionals

Demonstration of respect for diversity and tolerance for differences

Empathy for others

Use of sound ethical judgment

Ability to advocate for students with disabilities

Source: Framework adapted from *Case Studies in Assessment of Students with Disabilities* (pp. 3–7), by M. K. Weishaar & V. G. Scott, 2005, Boston: Allyn & Bacon.

Key Terms

child advocate
central auditory processing disorder

Cognitive Map to Guide Discussion
Chapter 2, Case 2.2: Sonya

Important Legal Issues Raised	Other Issues Raised
Subgroup of students in special education did not meet AYP on state test, resulting in schoolwide sanctions	How to improve curriculum and learning so that students in special education meet AYP
Safe harbor did not apply to subgroup of students in special education	Different special education teachers teaching same subject using different curricula and strategies
Determination of which students in special education should take the state test or the alternate state test	

Discussion—Foundation of Legal Issues and Other Issues Raised—Consider the Professional's:

Effective communication skills—verbal and written

Ability to self-reflect

Ability and willingness to collaborate with families and other professionals

Demonstration of respect for diversity and tolerance for differences

Empathy for others

Use of sound ethical judgment

Ability to advocate for students with disabilities

Source: Framework adapted from *Case Studies in Assessment of Students with Disabilities* (pp. 3–7), by M. K. Weishaar & V. G. Scott, 2005, Boston: Allyn & Bacon.

Key Terms

alternate assessment
adequate yearly progress (AYP)
safe harbor
subgroup
standard
individualized education program (IEP)
annual review

Cognitive Map to Guide Discussion
Chapter 3, Case 3.1: Tammy

Important Legal Issues Raised	Other Issues Raised
Determining which students in special education should take the state test	Exclusion of students in special education from the regular education environment
Systematic exclusion of students in special education from taking the state test	Self-esteem of student in special education who was excluded from taking the state test
Cheating to raise test scores	

Discussion—Foundation of Legal Issues and Other Issues Raised—Consider the Professional's:

Effective communication skills—verbal and written

Ability to self-reflect

Ability and willingness to collaborate with families and other professionals

Demonstration of respect for diversity and tolerance for differences

Empathy for others

Use of sound ethical judgment

Ability to advocate for students with disabilities

Source: Framework adapted from *Case Studies in Assessment of Students with Disabilities* (pp. 3–7), by M. K. Weishaar & V. G. Scott, 2005, Boston: Allyn & Bacon.

Key Terms

alternate assessment
state assessment
state standards
severe disability

Cognitive Map to Guide Discussion
Chapter 3, Case 3.2: Paul

Important Legal Issues Raised	Other Issues Raised
Transition plan	Functional/life skills curriculum vs. academic curriculum
Determination in IEP meeting if student in special education should take the state test and what accommodations, if any, are needed	Student with disability takes state test and lacks exposure to general education curriculum
Federal cap on the number of students with cognitive disabilities allowed to take an alternate assessment in lieu of the state assessment	Self-esteem of student with disability when faced with challenging assessment situation
	Progress of student with disability measured by state test vs. progress on IEP goals

Discussion—Foundation of Legal Issues and Other Issues Raised—Consider the Professional's:

Effective communication skills—verbal and written

Ability to self-reflect

Ability and willingness to collaborate with families and other professionals

Demonstration of respect for diversity and tolerance for differences

Empathy for others

Use of sound ethical judgment

Ability to advocate for students with disabilities

Source: Framework adapted from *Case Studies in Assessment of Students with Disabilities* (pp. 3–7), by M. K. Weishaar & V. G. Scott, 2005, Boston: Allyn & Bacon.

Key Terms

life skills
work-study program
annual IEP goal
Down syndrome
mild mental impairment
job coach

Cognitive Map to Guide Discussion
Chapter 4, Case 4.1: Jon

Important Legal Issues Raised	Other Issues Raised
Referral for an evaluation to determine eligibility for special education	Use of a prereferral intervention team (i.e., problem-solving team) to address early reading problems
Point at which the prereferral system becomes a referral for special education eligibility	Slow learner; consistent ability and achievement scores on standardized tests
Eligibility for learning disability; response to intervention vs. significant discrepancy between ability and achievement	Using research-based interventions and data-based methods of tracking progress

Discussion—Foundation of Legal Issues and Other Issues Raised—Consider the Professional's:

Effective communication skills—verbal and written

Ability to self-reflect

Ability and willingness to collaborate with families and other professionals

Demonstration of respect for diversity and tolerance for differences

Empathy for others

Use of sound ethical judgment

Ability to advocate for students with disabilities

Source: Framework adapted from *Case Studies in Assessment of Students with Disabilities* (pp. 3–7), by M. K. Weishaar & V. G. Scott, 2005, Boston: Allyn & Bacon.

Key Terms

learning disability
significant discrepancy between ability and achievement
problem-solving team
Dynamic Indicators of Basic Early Literacy Skills (DIBELS)
local education agency (LEA)
research-based intervention

Homework

Read information about DIBELS (*http://dibels.uoregon.edu*).

Cognitive Map to Guide Discussion
Chapter 4, Case 4.2: James

Important Legal Issues Raised	Other Issues Raised
Administrative decision to cease referrals to special education on an arbitrary date	Pressure on teachers in regular education to help students perform well on high-stakes tests
60-day time line to complete an evaluation for special education	Regular education teacher assuming total responsibility for a child's education if the child is not disabled
What constitutes a referral for a special education evaluation?	
Necessary participants on tteam conducting a special education evaluation	Administrative concern—lack of resources to provide personnel to conduct special education evaluations
Components of a special education evaluation	Lack of a prereferral intervention system

Discussion—Foundation of Legal Issues and Other Issues Raised—Consider the Professional's:
Effective communication skills—verbal and written

Ability to self-reflect

Ability and willingness to collaborate with families and other professionals

Demonstration of respect for diversity and tolerance for differences

Empathy for others

Use of sound ethical judgment

Ability to advocate for students with disabilities

Source: Framework adapted from *Case Studies in Assessment of Students with Disabilities* (pp. 3–7), by M. K. Weishaar & V. G. Scott, 2005, Boston: Allyn & Bacon.

Key Terms

adequate yearly progress (AYP)
Title I Reading
referral
evaluation

Cognitive Map to Guide Discussion
Chapter 5, Case 5.1: Brian

Important Legal Issues Raised	Other Issues Raised
Discipline of student previously evaluated, but not eligible for special education who made verbal threats	Security of school and safety of students
Extent of IDEA protection for student not currently identified as disabled	When does a verbal threat pose a safety issue for all students and adults in the school?
Extent to which school personnel "have knowledge" that student in question may be a student with a disability and implication of this knowledge	
Parent claim that student not in special education has a disability after the student is disciplined	

Discussion—Foundation of Legal Issues and Other Issues Raised—Consider the Professional's:

Effective communication skills—verbal and written

Ability to self-reflect

Ability and willingness to collaborate with families and other professionals

Demonstration of respect for diversity and tolerance for differences

Empathy for others

Use of sound ethical judgment

Ability to advocate for students with disabilities

Source: Framework adapted from *Case Studies in Assessment of Students with Disabilities* (pp. 3–7), by M. K. Weishaar & V. G. Scott, 2005, Boston: Allyn & Bacon.

Key Terms

expulsion
manifestation determination
expedited evaluation
referral
emotional disturbance

Cognitive Map to Guide Discussion
Chapter 5, Case 5.2: Terrance

Important Legal Issues Raised	Other Issues Raised
Suspension and possible expulsion of student with disability from school for possession of illegal drugs	Dual standard of consequences—possession of illegal drugs in the community vs. possession of illegal drugs at school
Conducting a manifestation determination	Dual standard of consequences—possession of illegal drugs by student with disability vs. possession of illegal drugs by student without disability
Extent to which local education agency is required to offer a free appropriate public education if student is expelled	

Discussion—Foundation of Legal Issues and Other Issues Raised—Consider the Professional's:

Effective communication skills—verbal and written

Ability to self-reflect

Ability and willingness to collaborate with families and other professionals

Demonstration of respect for diversity and tolerance for differences

Empathy for others

Use of sound ethical judgment

Ability to advocate for students with disabilities

Source: Framework adapted from *Case Studies in Assessment of Students with Disabilities* (pp. 3–7), by M. K. Weishaar & V. G. Scott, 2005, Boston: Allyn & Bacon.

Key Terms

functional behavioral assessment (FBA)
behavioral intervention plan (BIP)
manifestation determination
expulsion
suspension
interim alternative educational setting (IAES)
cross-categorical program
self-contained classroom
wraparound program

Homework

Read the following U.S. Supreme Court decision:

* *Honig v. Doe*, 479 U.S. 1084 (1988)

Cognitive Map to Guide Discussion
Chapter 6, Case 6.1: Carlos

Important Legal Issues Raised	Other Issues Raised
Accommodations were not documented in the IEP or properly determined by the IEP team	Accommodation decision was based on what was most convenient for the teacher
Accommodations were not appropriate (i.e., reading the reading test aloud)	There was an assumption that all instructional accommodations are appropriate for assessment
	There was an assumption that the same accommodations were appropriate for every student with disabilities

Discussion—Foundation of Legal Issues and Other Issues Raised—Consider the Professional's:

Effective communication skills—verbal and written

Ability to self-reflect

Ability and willingness to collaborate with families and other professionals

Demonstration of respect for diversity and tolerance for differences

Empathy for others

Use of sound ethical judgment

Ability to advocate for students with disabilities

Source: Framework adapted from *Case Studies in Assessment of Students with Disabilities* (pp. 3–7), by M. K. Weishaar & V. G. Scott, 2005, Boston: Allyn & Bacon.

Key Terms

accommodation
adequate yearly progress (AYP)
individualized education program (IEP)

Homework

Study the manual developed by the Council of Chief State School Officers (CCSSO): *Accommodations Manual: How to Select, Administer, and Evaluate Use of Accommodations for Instruction and Assessment of Students with Disabilities* (2nd ed., 2005), available online at the Web site of the CCSSO (*http://www.ccsso.org/content/pdfs/AccommodationsManual.pdf*).

Cognitive Map to Guide Discussion
Chapter 6, Case 6.2: Anna

Important Legal Issues Raised	Other Issues Raised
Eligibility for learning disability based on significant discrepancy and lack of response to intervention	Assessment to track progress—for example, Dynamic Indicators of Basic Early Literacy Skills (DIBELS)
Parent consent for an evaluation: When should it occur when using response to intervention (RtI) as part of the evaluation?	Definition of learning disability
Parent participation	Standardized intelligence and achievement testing

Discussion—Foundation of Legal Issues and Other Issues Raised—Consider the Professional's:

Effective communication skills—verbal and written

Ability to self-reflect

Ability and willingness to collaborate with families and other professionals

Demonstration of respect for diversity and tolerance for differences

Empathy for others

Use of sound ethical judgment

Ability to advocate for students with disabilities

Source: Framework adapted from *Case Studies in Assessment of Students with Disabilities* (pp. 3–7), by M. K. Weishaar & V. G. Scott, 2005, Boston: Allyn & Bacon.

Key Terms

response to intervention (RtI)
significant discrepancy
phonemic awareness
reading fluency
phonics

Homework

Study the manual developed by the Council of Chief State School Officers (CCSSO): *Accommodations Manual: How to Select, Administer, and Evaluate Use of Accommodations for Instruction and Assessment of Students with Disabilities* (2nd ed., 2005), available online at the Web site of the CCSSO (*http://www.ccsso.org/content/pdfs/AccommodationsManual.pdf*).

Cognitive Map to Guide Discussion
Chapter 7, Case 7.1: Thomas

Important Legal Issues Raised	Other Issues Raised
IEP appropriate to meet the student's individual needs	Academic vs. life skills or functional curriculum for student with significant disabilities
Appropriate transition plan	Grading based on effort rather than outcomes
Appropriateness of Thomas participating in the state test with accommodations	Self-esteem of student with significant disability
Potential consequences of Thomas's state test results	

Discussion—Foundation of Legal Issues and Other Issues Raised—Consider the Professional's:

Effective communication skills—verbal and written

Ability to self-reflect

Ability and willingness to collaborate with families and other professionals

Demonstration of respect for diversity and tolerance for differences

Empathy for others

Use of sound ethical judgment

Ability to advocate for students with disabilities

Source: Framework adapted from *Case Studies in Assessment of Students with Disabilities* (pp. 3–7), by M. K. Weishaar & V. G. Scott, 2005, Boston: Allyn & Bacon.

Key Terms

annual review

transition

seizure

significant cognitive delay

retinal degeneration

visual impairment

central auditory processing disorder

speech and language delay

educational benefit

Braille

least restrictive environment (LRE)

Homework

Read the following U.S. Supreme Court decision:

* *Board of Education of the Hendrick Hudson School District v. Rowley,* 458 U.S. 176 (1982)

Cognitive Map to Guide Discussion
Chapter 7, Case 7.2: Jacob

Important Legal Issues Raised	Other Issues Raised
Extent to which the IEP should reflect methodology	Conflict resolution
Extent to which the parent can dictate methodology used in the classroom	
Extent to which the school must develop the child to meet the "full potential" vs. providing appropriate services so that the child can make reasonable progress	

Discussion—Foundation of Legal Issues and Other Issues Raised—Consider the Professional's:

Effective communication skills—verbal and written
Ability to self-reflect
Ability and willingness to collaborate with families and other professionals
Demonstration of respect for diversity and tolerance for differences
Empathy for others
Use of sound ethical judgment
Ability to advocate for students with disabilities

Source: Framework adapted from *Case Studies in Assessment of Students with Disabilities* (pp. 3–7), by M. K. Weishaar & V. G. Scott, 2005, Boston: Allyn & Bacon.

Key Terms

applied behavioral analysis (ABA) therapy
autism
pervasive developmental delay
occupational therapy
speech-language therapy
discrete trial training
picture exchange communication system (PECS)
due process hearing

Homework

Read the following U.S. Supreme Court decision:

* *Board of Education of the Hendrick Hudson School District v. Rowley*, 458 U.S. 176 (1982)

Cognitive Map to Guide Discussion
Chapter 8, Case 8.1: Rhonda

Important Legal Issues Raised	Other Issues Raised
Regular education teacher's refusal to follow the IEP	Conflict resolution
Free appropriate public education (FAPE) for Rhonda in the least restrictive environment (LRE)	Communication between professionals
Appropriate and individualized IEP	Collaboration between regular education teacher and special education teacher
	Who is responsible for the education of a child with a disability?

Discussion—Foundation of Legal Issues and Other Issues Raised—Consider the Professional's:

Effective communication skills—verbal and written

Ability to self-reflect

Ability and willingness to collaborate with families and other professionals

Demonstration of respect for diversity and tolerance for differences

Empathy for others

Use of sound ethical judgment

Ability to advocate for students with disabilities

Source: Framework adapted from *Case Studies in Assessment of Students with Disabilities* (pp. 3–7), by M. K. Weishaar & V. G. Scott, 2005, Boston: Allyn & Bacon.

Key Terms

evaluation

adaptation

accommodation

self-contained special education class

learning disability

Homework

Read the following U.S. court decisions:

* *Board of Education of the Hendrick Hudson School District v. Rowley*, 458 U.S. 176 (1982)
* *Daniel R. R. v. State Board of Education*, 874 F.2d 1036 (5th Cir. 1989)
* *Greer v. Rome City School District*, 950 F.2d 688 (11th Cir. 1991)
* *Sacramento City Unified School District Board of Education v. Rachel H.*, 14 F.3d 1398 (9th Cir. 1994)

Cognitive Map to Guide Discussion
Chapter 8, Case 8.2: Jameca

Important Legal Issues Raised	Other Issues Raised
Parental input into IEP development	Conflict resolution
Placement of student with significant behavior problems in a public high school vs. off-campus treatment center	Placement of student with significant behavior problems in a class where there are positive role models (regular high school) vs. day treatment center where there are more negative role models
Transition	Student earning right (via appropriate behavior) to be placed in regular high school
	Once a student is placed into special education, the student never returns to regular education

Discussion—Foundation of Legal Issues and Other Issues Raised—Consider the Professional's:

Effective communication skills—verbal and written

Ability to self-reflect

Ability and willingness to collaborate with families and other professionals

Demonstration of respect for diversity and tolerance for differences

Empathy for others

Use of sound ethical judgment

Ability to advocate for students with disabilities

Source: Framework adapted from *Case Studies in Assessment of Students with Disabilities* (pp. 3–7), by M. K. Weishaar & V. G. Scott, 2005, Boston: Allyn & Bacon.

Key Terms

day treatment facility
accommodation
resource programming
emotional disturbance
behavior disorder (BD)
present levels of performance
supplementary aids and services

Cognitive Map to Guide Discussion
Chapter 9, Case 9.1: Darnell

Important Legal Issues Raised	Other Issues Raised
Removal of student from school property without parent knowledge	Police administering discipline for school
Principal's role in administering discipline for child with an IEP	Principal's right to protect other children's rights to learn in a safe environment
Suspension from school for more than 30 days	
Expulsion from school for the remainder of the school year	

Discussion—Foundation of Legal Issues and Other Issues Raised—Consider the Professional's:

Effective communication skills—verbal and written

Ability to self-reflect

Ability and willingness to collaborate with families and other professionals

Demonstration of respect for diversity and tolerance for differences

Empathy for others

Use of sound ethical judgment

Ability to advocate for students with disabilities

Source: Framework adapted from *Case Studies in Assessment of Students with Disabilities* (pp. 3–7), by M. K. Weishaar & V. G. Scott, 2005, Boston: Allyn & Bacon.

Key Terms

due process hearing
resolution meeting
mediation
behavior management plan
manifestation determination

Cognitive Map to Guide Discussion
Chapter 9, Case 9.2: Andrew

Important Legal Issues Raised	Other Issues Raised
Parent input into IEP	Conflict resolution
Appropriate and individualized IEP	Data-based decision-making
Procedure used to develop IEP	Family stress
Consent for placement vs. signing the IEP	Communication between home and school
Observation by parent's independent evaluator	

Discussion—Foundation of Legal Issues and Other Issues Raised—Consider the Professional's:

Effective communication skills—verbal and written

Ability to self-reflect

Ability and willingness to collaborate with families and other professionals

Demonstration of respect for diversity and tolerance for differences

Empathy for others

Use of sound ethical judgment

Ability to advocate for students with disabilities

Source: Framework adapted from *Case Studies in Assessment of Students with Disabilities* (pp. 3–7), by M. K. Weishaar & V. G. Scott, 2005, Boston: Allyn & Bacon.

Key Terms

IEP meeting
free appropriate public education (FAPE)

Cognitive Map to Guide Discussion
Chapter 10, Case 10.1: Dan

Important Legal Issues Raised	Other Issues Raised
Predetermining services provided outside of the IEP meeting	Providing assessment data to the parent prior to an IEP meeting
Individualized IEP goals	Communication between home and school
Meaningful parental input into the IEP and eligibility decisions	
Informed consent for special education services	

Discussion—Foundation of Legal Issues and Other Issues Raised—Consider the Professional's:

Effective communication skills—verbal and written

Ability to self-reflect

Ability and willingness to collaborate with families and other professionals

Demonstration of respect for diversity and tolerance for differences

Empathy for others

Use of sound ethical judgment

Ability to advocate for students with disabilities

Source: Framework adapted from *Case Studies in Assessment of Students with Disabilities* (pp. 3–7), by M. K. Weishaar & V. G. Scott, 2005, Boston: Allyn & Bacon.

Key Terms

IQ
general achievement
discrepancy
phonemic awareness
present levels of performance
IEP goals
accommodation

Cognitive Map to Guide Discussion
Chapter 10, Case 10.2: Maria

Important Legal Issues Raised	Other Issues Raised
Changing an IEP without convening an IEP meeting or gaining written consent from the parent to change the IEP without a meeting	Data-based decision-making
	Communication between home and school
Individualizing the IEP—providing related services based on the child's need, not the convenience of the provider	

Discussion—Foundation of Legal Issues and Other Issues Raised—Consider the Professional's:

Effective communication skills—verbal and written

Ability to self-reflect

Ability and willingness to collaborate with families and other professionals

Demonstration of respect for diversity and tolerance for differences

Empathy for others

Use of sound ethical judgment

Ability to advocate for students with disabilities

Source: Framework adapted from *Case Studies in Assessment of Students with Disabilities* (pp. 3–7), by M. K. Weishaar & V. G. Scott, 2005, Boston: Allyn & Bacon.

Key Terms

IEP meeting

individual pull-out services

IEP conference summary

Index